DEMYSTIFYING OUTSOURCING

The Trainer's Guide to Working with Vendors and Consultants

Debbie Friedman

Pfeiffer

A Wiley Imprint

www.pfeiffer.com

Library of Congress Cataloging-in-Publication Data
Friedman, Debbie
   Demystifying outsourcing : the trainer's guide to working with vendors and consultants / Debbie Friedman.
      p. cm.
   Includes bibliographical references and index.
   ISBN-13: 978-0-7879-7941-6 (pbk.)
   ISBN-10: 0-7879-7941-4 (pbk.)
   1. Contracting out-Handbooks, manuals, etc. I. Title.
   HD2365.F75 2006
   658.4'058—dc22   2006008662

Acquiring Editor: Martin Delahoussaye   Production Editor: Dawn Kilgore
Director of Development: Kathleen Dolan Davies Editor: Rebecca Taff
Developmental Editor: Susan Rachmeler   Manufacturing Supervisor: Becky Carreño
Printed in the United States of America

Printing   10 9 8 7 6 5 4 3 2 1

About This Book

Why is this topic important?

There has been a rapid increase in outsourcing in the field of training and development. Often training managers are required to outsource complex projects in areas in which they may have little expertise. The risks are great. Quality, reputation, and significant financial resources are at stake. Today's business climate of budgetary constraints and higher demands by management for training organizations to deliver results that impact the bottom line create even greater pressures. Since the stakes are high, it is critical to minimize the risks in the outsourcing equation. The differential between a successful outsourced project and one that is not is a highly skilled training manager, an individual who knows how to work effectively with training vendors and consultants.

What can you achieve with this book?

This book has been written to demystify outsourcing and the relationship between training managers and their outsourcing partners. Training managers can use this book to expand their capabilities as outsourcing partners as they expand the capabilities of their departments. Their outsourced initiatives will help expand the capabilities of their organizations. The book responds to the question, "How can training mangers take a strategic approach, successfully manage outsourced projects, and achieve objectives while maintaining outsourcing partnerships?" External consultants will also find value. They will gain a greater understanding of the role of training managers, the pressures they face, and how best to build partnerships. Training managers and consultants will achieve maximum benefit if they jointly utilize the tools and worksheets that have been provided. Using the personal learning journal that is threaded throughout the book will help the training manager grow as an outsourcing partner.

How is the book organized?

Part One of this book examines trends in outsourcing and introduces guiding principles that should govern every outsourced project. It explores the need to take a strategic approach, the importance of developing strong partnerships, and the value of continuous learning. It also introduces a strategic decision model for sourcing that enables managers to make wise choices about what to outsource and what to retain. Parts Two and Three guide managers through the phases of a project. These sections provide numerous examples, advice, practical tools, and techniques that can be applied to any outsourced projects. Part Four covers special topics, such as managing conflict and the challenges of working with multiple consultants. Part Five helps training managers build a development plan to expand their capabilities as an outsourcing partner.

A special feature of this book is a CD. It includes worksheets that guide the training manager and consultant step-by-step through a project, samples, and the Personal Learning Journal. A CD icon indicates that the resource is available on the CD. You can customize these tools.

About Pfeiffer

Pfeiffer serves the professional development and hands-on resource needs of training and human resource practitioners and gives them products to do their jobs better. We deliver proven ideas and solutions from experts in HR development and HR management, and we offer effective and customizable tools to improve workplace performance. From novice to seasoned professional, Pfeiffer is the source you can trust to make yourself and your organization more successful.

Essential Knowledge Pfeiffer produces insightful, practical, and comprehensive materials on topics that matter the most to training and HR professionals. Our Essential Knowledge resources translate the expertise of seasoned professionals into practical, how-to guidance on critical workplace issues and problems. These resources are supported by case studies, worksheets, and job aids and are frequently supplemented with CD-ROMs, websites, and other means of making the content easier to read, understand, and use.

Essential Tools Pfeiffer's Essential Tools resources save time and expense by offering proven, ready-to-use materials—including exercises, activities, games, instruments, and assessments—for use during a training or team-learning event. These resources are frequently offered in looseleaf or CD-ROM format to facilitate copying and customization of the material.

Pfeiffer also recognizes the remarkable power of new technologies in expanding the reach and effectiveness of training. While e-hype has often created whizbang solutions in search of a problem, we are dedicated to bringing convenience and enhancements to proven training solutions. All our e-tools comply with rigorous functionality standards. The most appropriate technology wrapped around essential content yields the perfect solution for today's on-the-go trainers and human resource professionals.

www.pfeiffer.com

Essential resources for training and HR professionals

To
Esther
who helped me take the road less traveled
and to
Jeff and Lisa
who supported me along the way.

Contents

List of Exhibits, Figures, and Tables

Contents of the CD-ROM

Learning Journal

Foreword

Richard was tall, dark, and handsome; I was none of these. Richard called the CEO "Tom" as if they were old buddies; protocol dictated I always inserted "Mister" in front of the top leader's last name, like every other officer of the bank. Richard had a quiet confidence and an easy manner; I was noisy and irreverent. And when Richard spoke to a group of senior executives from his Ph.D. expertise and his "been there-done that" depth, they listened as if he were straight from Mount Olympus. I hated Richard!

Well, maybe "hate" is too strong a label. I was a new training director; Richard was the industrial psychologist hired by the president to "help" with executive and organization development. I watched Richard frequently enter sanctums on mahogany row that I rarely was allowed to visit. My recommendations spoken from his lips were somehow suddenly valued by the movers and shakers. Like the lyrics of the old country song, I came to wonder, "Tell me what's he got that I ain't got."

Our story had a happy ending. Richard and I became great friends, respectful colleagues, and ultimately partners in a consulting firm we helped create. My resentment was transformed into mutual respect; his guruism turned into collaboration. The path to that evolution is what *Demystifying Outsourcing* is all about. Every day in the corporate world, an internal professional wrestles with the decisions of whether and how to choose a Richard and, more importantly, how to collaborate with a Richard.

Important lessons need not be learned in the school of hard knocks. I was fortunate to have a manager who played the role that Debbie Friedman now plays for you in this valuable book. Watching me struggle with my bruised ego, my boss coached me to focus on my professional standards, not on my popularity standing. After I shared with him some "Richard bashing" hearsay, he advised me to assume the best in Richard and trust my experience, not water cooler scuttlebutt. Once Dr. Richard experienced my obvious professional respect and cut-to-the-chase candor, we were able to forge a partnership that produced work that made a difference.

Demystifying Outsourcing is the all-inclusive toolkit on how to plan, grow, and nurture a bountiful professional partnership. However, this toolkit comes with a lot of extras—unexpected resources designed to take the scary out of the process. Far more than a tome to help you make smart decisions, it is crafted in a form that leaves you a much smarter decision-maker. It elevates the client-consultant relationship to one of synergy, not symbiosis; one that enriches the lives of the partners, not just enhances the outcome of the project. And, while the primary target is the training director's outsourcing journey, *Demystifying Outsourcing* serves as valuable counsel for managing all relationships that matter.

My Debbie Friedman—the boss who gave me important "Richard-handling lessons"—told me I'd be prudent to approach a professional relationship like a smart farmer approaches growing a first-rate crop—a lot of planning and preparation precedes planting seeds; a lot of weeding and pruning goes on after the plants come up; and a lot of care and conservation ensures the land will be ready for next year's harvest.

Demystifying Outsourcing is divided into these same three parts. Strategic sourcing is the planning and preparation crucial to effective outsourcing.

Farmers do not plant crops just anywhere; they strategically pick planting sites effectively aligned with all nature can offer. Wise training directors plan outsourcing with similar forethought. They align projects with people; project objectives with organizational priorities, and sources with strategy. Smart farmers pick healthy seeds appropriate to the locale. Smart training directors choose consultants who fit. The alignment process is far more than a "talent contest." It is the thoughtful management of a myriad of factors to turn an adequate decision into one laced with prudence and promise.

Transforming partnerships—the second step in the process—includes the "weeding and pruning" of the client-consultant relationship needed to nurture a necessary liaison into a valuable partnership. Transforming partnerships—that is, partnerships that are transformational—inspire and motivate. They are those confederations that conduct themselves with such health and fullness they signal to struggling alliances that greatness is possible. They are the "works in progress" that show others that change—organizational, interpersonal, and personal—is all about growth. Grounded in such sustaining virtues as trust, honesty, and generosity, Friedman provides the rakes, hoes, fertilizer, and most importantly, the "whisper in your ear" mentoring that can take a consulting partnership to new heights and rich bounty. Like a master consultant, she provides the enabling methods and "do-it-yourself" tools.

Harvesting to a farmer is more than gathering crops for storage in the barn. It is about the care and maintenance that ensures the soil and equipment will return an even more productive crop the next season. Wise project planners continue to "sharpen the plow." They reflect on the past to refine the future; they seek feedback to feed forward. They nurture networks to deepen influence and expand inclusion. They build sponsorships and reinforce organizational anchors. They care more about long-term sustainability than simply completing an objective. Integration is more a critical success factor than implementation.

This book can serve you in many ways. It is an instruction manual, an apparatus for professional soul searching, and a powerful reference tool. Please do not read it like the college text you scanned or the novel you raced through just to get to the "good part." Read it thoughtfully; complete the workbook parts introspectively; and return to it repeatedly like a wise friend with limitless counsel relevant most when you are ready it hear it.

Demystifying Outsourcing embraces a vital philosophy: when it comes to ball games, it's not over 'til it's over; when it comes to growing capability, it is never, ever over. The project may end and the consultant may exit, but organizational improvement is a perpetual journey. That journey is made easier, more rewarding, and far more abundant because of the important gift you now hold in your hands.

Chip Bell

Preface

When I first started to work with vendors and consultants, I was overwhelmed. There seemed to be so much at stake—the budget, my reputation, my career. Early on, I ended up in a difficult situation, having selected the wrong vendor for a high-profile project. It was six weeks before the launch of a senior leadership program, and I had to dismiss the vendor. Thank goodness for a supportive boss. Somehow luck was on our side. I found an extraordinary consultant, who is still one of our partners today, and we successfully launched our program.

There were other projects, some that went smoothly and some that did not. I was often not sure what direction to take. I did not understand the value of building true partnerships. I was lucky again. The consultants were patient with me.

Over time, I noticed that projects started to go more smoothly. I had learned some things along the way. I began to feel more confident, and that caused me to have more positive interactions with vendors and consultants. I looked forward to working with them, because of everything I would learn. I also enjoyed them as individuals and began to value their partnership. I began to see my role differently. In the same way that they were there to help me and my company be successful, my role was to help them be successful. What used to be the most difficult part of my job became the most enjoyable. I began to think about writing a book to help other training professionals learn ways to work more effectively with vendors and consultants. I wanted to share with others what took me many years to learn.

The writing of this book has been a transforming experience. It has given me the opportunity to strengthen existing partnerships. It has also opened me up to new and unexpected partnerships. The generosity of spirit that my colleagues have demonstrated has been one of the most special experiences of my life. In the process I have learned yet again that the greatest blessing of life is the connections we make with each other.

Debbie Friedman

June 2006

Acknowledgments

This book is about transforming partnerships. As I wrote the book, I reached out to colleagues for ideas and support. The partnerships I developed transformed the content; and in the process, I was transformed. I am deeply touched and wish to express my gratitude to the many people who demonstrated a spirit of generosity.

Joyce Chavkin, my sister, a former English teacher and writing coach, spent hours with me on the phone reviewing my manuscript. Our conversations were laced with personal stories about our jobs, our kids, and our mom. We got to know each other on an entirely different level, which deepened my love and respect for her. I cherish her gentle feedback and support.

Martin Delahoussaye, my editor, took a chance on a new author. What a delightful partner I found in Martin. He challenged my thinking and gave honest feedback while always reassuring me along the way. His wisdom helped me strengthen this book.

Susan Smyth, my friend and colleague, was instrumental in helping me get started. She co-authored the proposal, introduced me to Martin Delahoussaye at Pfeiffer, interviewed several colleagues, and deepened my understanding of partnerships.

David Giber, senior vice president at Linkage Incorporated, supported this project from the outset. David's unparalleled creativity and spirit of generosity have helped me build outstanding executive development programs at Federated. He served as a sounding board, read my manuscript, and gave exceptional feedback. Many of the tips and tools have come from lessons I have learned through my partnership with David.

Rusty Sullivan, author, attorney at Linkage Incorporated, and executive director of the Sports Museum in Boston, co-authored the sections on RFPs and contracts. Rusty and I have a virtual partnership. We have never met in person. He gave his precious time while starting a new job to ensure that these two sections of the book were legally defensible, while reflecting a true spirit of partnership.

Rob Goldberg of Organization Insight, writer and consultant extraordinaire, has taught me so much through our years of collaboration. He read the earliest drafts of the manuscript and, as usual, gave me feedback that brought the book to a more sophisticated level. I am always amazed by Rob's grasp of the nuance of language. Thank you for sharing your expertise with me.

Colleague and friend Joann Jones, Vice President-Talent Management and OD, ServiceMaster, is an outstanding organization development professional. We spent hours on the phone and got to know each other better, personally and professionally. The most enjoyable times were our virtual dinners by cell phone, sharing a glass of wine and exchanging ideas about the book. I greatly appreciate the time she took away from Emma and Don to review the manuscript and give me excellent feedback.

Over coffee at Awakenings, Keith Burtoft of Markers & Mice helped me clarify my thinking about the key principles of the book. With his sharp mind, there were times when I was sure Keith understood what I was trying to say better than I did. After our meetings, I would anxiously await his follow-up emails. The attachments were always so exciting to open. There I would discover how he creatively translated my ideas into art.

Sherry Hollock, my boss and partner for the last nineteen years, made this book possible. Not only did she support my writing, but she also created an atmosphere in which I could learn and grow. Sherry taught me about partnerships in which team members drive hard for results while caring about people.

Research for this book included numerous interviews with OD/training experts in the field. These interviews brought a greater richness to the text and were the source of many of the stories. My thanks go to Merrill Anderson (MetrixGlobal, LLC), Peter Block (Designed Learning), Brandon Hall (Brandon Hall Research), Doug Harward (TrainingOutsourcing.com, LLC), Larry Kahn (LH KAHN), Jacques Labrie (Development Dimensions International/DDI Canada), Corey Leverette (Centurion Systems, Inc.), Mike Lair (Lair Learning Alliance), Leslie Mc Cleary (The Children's Place), Steve McMillan (Hillenbrand Industries), Fred Meyer (Fred Meyer & Associates), Peter Mulford (BTS), Sheryl Riddle (Development Dimensions International, Inc./DDI), Bob Riess (Innovative Training Services, LLC), Dana Robinson (Partners in Change, Inc.), and Tim Rooks (Federated Department Stores).

A wise person once told me that you are lucky if you have one or two special friends in a lifetime. I have been lucky. Sandey Fields and Ophra Weisberg define friendship. They have been my greatest supporters in good times and bad. I am very grateful.

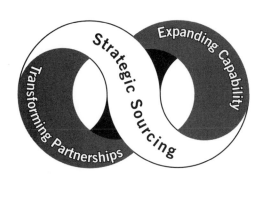

Part 1

Building a Strategic Foundation

Chapter 1   Introduction
Chapter 2   Guiding Principles
Chapter 3   Sourcing: A Strategic Decision

PART 1 begins with an exploration of organizational trends that have caused an increase in outsourcing in training and development. It examines the risks and benefits of outsourcing and then lays a foundation through a discussion of three guiding principles—strategic sourcing, transforming partnerships, and expanding capability. This part ends with the introduction of a strategic sourcing decision model that helps training managers determine which initiatives to outsource and which to retain.

Introduction

The Growth of Outsourcing

Outsourcing is not a new phenomenon. For years training managers have engaged keynote speakers for conferences and contracted for design, delivery, and evaluation of training programs. More recently they have outsourced executive coaching, benchmarking, culture change initiatives, and the development of enterprise-wide learning systems. There are even a small, but growing, number of firms that have outsourced their entire training function.

Recent studies confirm the rise of outsourcing.

- ASTD's *2005 State of the Industry Report* shows a steady increase in the percentage of learning expenditures that go to outside services, from an average of 20 percent in 1999 to 27 percent in 2004, with an expected increase to 29 percent in 2005 (Sugrue & Rivera, 2005).

- *Training* magazine's 2005 Industry Report indicates that the percentage of organizations that outsourced some of the design of their traditional training (as opposed to technology-based training) rose from 35 percent to 38 percent over the previous year. Of all the organizations that outsourced technology-based training, 35 percent outsourced some of the delivery, an increase of 4 percent over the previous year, and almost 44 percent outsourced some of the development of this training, a 3 percent increase over the previous year (Dolezalek, 2005).

- Corporate, government, and other organizations are turning toward training outsourcing in record numbers. The field is currently growing at a 15 percent clip, compared with an 8 percent rate for the training marketplace overall (Harris, 2004, p. 36).

Why Outsourcing Is Increasing

Factors have converged to make the field ripe for more outsourcing. Organizations today face challenges such as:

- Volatile economic conditions
- Globalization
- Increased competition
- Technological advances
- Mergers and acquisitions
- Need for greater speed and reduction in cycle time
- More knowledgeable customers with higher expectations
- Greater diversity among employees
- Gaps in the leadership pipeline

These pressures have caused shifts in organizational strategy, business processes, and systems. The cultural implications are enormous as employees adapt to the magnitude of change. How do these trends impact training and development and lead to increased outsourcing? What other issues have contributed?

Increased Demand Due to Organizational Change

Senior leaders recognize that it takes knowledgeable employees to respond to all the change. In a newly merged company, managers must learn to lead larger teams as their areas of responsibility expand. The need to reduce cycle time requires employees to learn new business processes and systems. Increased diversity may mean that employees must learn to manage conflict. The result is an increase in requests for training.

Training, once on the periphery, has been elevated in many organizations to a key business strategy. Leaders recognize that training professionals are important business partners, and training is needed for the organization to realize its objectives. Yet years of downsizing have left training departments operating with limited resources. There are too many projects and not enough time. The response is to outsource, expanding the capability of the training department and enabling it to meet the needs of the line organization in a timely fashion.

Advances in Technology

It is not only the *number* of projects that have caused more outsourcing, but also the *nature* of the projects. With advances in technology, more training programs are technology-based. The internal trainer may not have the expertise to develop a technology-based solution. Due to cost, the organization may be reluctant to build internal capability to do this type of course development. Advances in technology have also made learning management systems (LMSs) readily available for administrative functions such as registration and tracking. The purchase of an LMS is comparable to making an enterprise-wide software decision, a decision that may be beyond the capabilities of the average training manager.

Need for Expertise

When tracing outsourcing decisions, it is not uncommon to discover that the staff of the training department may not be prepared to solve certain organizational problems. With the pace of change, new training managers are sometimes forced to operate at sophisticated levels before they have ample opportunity to develop in-depth knowledge of the field. Resources are limited. Under these conditions, it is natural to outsource the development of a senior leadership program or a comprehensive evaluation project. One of the benefits of outsourcing is that involvement with external consultants helps build the capability of the training organization.

A training department may choose to outsource even if there is a staff of highly skilled training professionals. For example, a manufacturing company commits to an organization-wide process improvement program. There are significant training needs to support this strategic initiative. Although a top performer, the training manager does not have the required expertise. The best decision may be outsourcing.

Need for External Perspective

There are times when an external and objective perspective would benefit the organization. For example, it is usually best for a consultant to facilitate a team meeting for the top leadership of an organization. The training manager, even if highly regarded, would probably have difficulty confronting the issues in the same way an external consultant could. There would be too much at stake from a political standpoint for the internal and less risk for the external.

Cost Savings

Outsourcing can help organizations reduce expenses, gain efficiencies, and focus on the core business. For years organizations have outsourced human resource functions viewed as non-core, particularly benefits and compensation. Because training is about people, who are the core of most businesses, there has been a reluctance to do large-scale outsourcing in this area.

However, to reduce cost and gain efficiencies, large-scale outsourcing in training is beginning in administrative areas, including registration, tracking, evaluation, and operations. Rather than making large investments in technology, outsourcing providers let the organization pay as it goes, fronting the money and getting it back in fees over the life of the contract (Hall, 2004).

A small number of organizations have outsourced the entire training function, including design, development, and delivery. In large-scale outsourcing, trainers often shift employers and begin working for the outsourcing provider. An individual or a team remains to work in partnership with the external provider to manage the outsourcing relationship. Large-scale outsourcing has enabled organizations to reduce headcount and save payroll expense.

Benefits Outweigh the Risks

Training managers who outsource face considerable political and financial risk. They may make poor consultant or vendor selections. They may inadequately prepare consultants to work in their organizations. Consultants may be unable to establish credibility with management or develop programs that fit the culture. IT partners may refuse to implement a vendor's technology-based solution, because they were not involved sufficiently in project planning. There are many pitfalls, and projects can easily go awry.

Although the risks are significant, outsourcing brings significant organizational and personal benefits to those who do it well. Organizations benefit through:

- *Thought leadership:* Access to the latest thinking about learning methodologies, the best demonstrated practices in the field of learning and successful outsourcing strategies

- *Reduction in cycle time for developing learning:* Ability for learning professionals to deliver faster results to their internal business clients

- *Access to greater objectivity:* Ability of the external provider, less influenced by internal politics, to render more objective assessments and develop learning that will meet these needs

- *Reduction of fixed costs:* Ability of an organization to increase or decrease outsourcing depending on business conditions, allowing the organization to operate with smaller permanent staffs who can feel greater job security (Anderson, 2000).

Training managers who outsource typically grow as professionals. While expanding the capabilities of their departments through outsourcing, they expand their personal capabilities. They have the opportunity to learn new content and approaches. In the outsourcing partnership, they often learn skills that help them interact more effectively with senior management and make change happen more successfully in their organizations. They also can learn to become better business partners as they collaborate with their external vendors and consultants. Outsourced initiatives are usually breeding grounds for rich development experiences.

Although the benefits of outsourcing are significant, the stakes are high. It is critical to minimize the risks in the outsourcing equation. The differential between a successful outsourced project and one that is not is a highly skilled training manager, an individual who can make wise outsourcing choices and who can successfully manage outsourced projects.

Purpose of This Book

Although there are numerous books written to teach external consultants how to work more effectively with their internal training partners, very little is written to teach training managers the skills needed to successfully manage complex projects when external consultants are involved.

This book has been written to demystify outsourcing and the relationship between training managers and their outsourcing partners. It will strengthen the skills and build the confidence of training managers who outsource. They will learn how to navigate complex projects, working effectively with vendors and consultants to achieve results.

The book is about expanding capability on many levels. Training managers who utilize the book can expand their capabilities as outsourcing partners.

Through outsourcing, they can expand the capabilities of their departments. Finally, their outsourced initiatives help expand the capabilities of their organizations.

The book has broader application and will be helpful to any professional who seeks the services of outside vendors and consultants to help solve organizational problems. These might include human resource managers, internal organization development consultants, purchasing managers, information technology professionals, and any business manager who is involved in outsourcing. External consultants will find value as well. They will gain a greater understanding of the role of managers, the pressures they face, and how best to build partnerships. Finally, students and faculty in the fields of human resources, training, psychology, and business will get a glimpse into organizational life and a head start developing capabilities required for future success.

An Overview of This Book

This book responds to the question, "How can training managers take a strategic approach to outsourcing, successfully manage outsourced projects, and achieve objectives while maintaining outsourcing partnerships?" As a comprehensive toolkit, it provides principles, practical tips, and tools to build the self-confidence and skills of training managers.

Part 1 builds the foundation. It introduces current trends in outsourcing and guiding principles that should govern every outsourced project. This section also introduces a strategic sourcing decision model to help managers make wise choices about what to outsource and what to retain.

Parts 2 and 3 guide managers step-by-step through an outsourced project, from identifying potential outsourcing partners and negotiating contracts through design, delivery, and program evaluation. With an emphasis on creating true partnerships, these sections provide numerous examples, advice, practical tools, and techniques that can be applied to any outsourced project.

Part 4 discusses special situations in outsourcing, such as how to deal with conflict, inheriting a consultant, and working with multiple consultants.

Part 5 assists managers in summarizing what they have learned and helps them build a development plan to expand their capabilities as an outsourcing partner.

Numerous stories bring the challenges of outsourcing to light. All are true. They are based on the experiences of the author and several of her colleagues, both internal training managers and external consultants. Because these professionals did not want their names and their organizations revealed, this information has been kept confidential.

How You Can Use This Book

This book is a flexible resource. Worksheets and samples are provided on the accompanying CD to help advance your projects and partnerships. The CD icon indicates that a resource is available on the CD. These can be tailored to the needs of any project. Most worksheets are designed to be completed jointly with your outsourcing partners.

If you are relatively new to outsourcing, you will probably want to follow the book in a linear fashion. Use it as a guidebook as you work through the phases of an outsourced project. If you are further along on a project, go directly to the section of the book that is most relevant. In either case, you may want to provide a copy of the book to your outsourcing partners.

If you are experienced, begin with Chapters 2 and 3 to get a sense of the philosophy of outsourcing that is presented. You will probably find Chapter 3, which contains the Strategic Sourcing Decision Model, particularly interesting. It will help you reflect on the quality of previous sourcing decisions you have made and will be useful in making future decisions. Then review the chapters that you believe will be most valuable to your future outsourcing.

If you are an external consultant, you might consider this book as a gift to clients. It would make a strong statement about the value you place on developing partnerships.

Threaded throughout the book is a personal learning journal. It is also available on the enclosed CD. If your goal is to expand your capabilities as an outsourcing partner, the learning journal will help you reflect on what you have learned and will support you in building a development plan for out-sourcing success.

A Few Definitions

Before proceeding, it is helpful to define some terms that are used in this book.

Outsourcing is defined as obtaining the services of an external provider to solve an organizational problem. That service could have been performed by personnel within the organization. However, the organization decides it is better to contract for services from the outside in order to reduce costs, save time, or gain expertise or objectivity.

Out-tasking refers to hiring an external provider on a limited basis to do a particular project, such as design or delivery of a training program. Today many training professionals have begun to use the term out-tasking to differentiate it from large-scale outsourcing, when a firm takes complete responsibility for and control of selected learning processes or takes over the entire training function (DeViney & Sugrue, 2004).

Since most professionals still use the term outsourcing, whether the initiative is large or small, outsourcing will be used in this book regardless of the size of the initiative.

Training managers is used for the sake of simplicity to represent all job titles in the field of training, organization development, and human resources. It encompasses new job titles, such as learning specialist and performance consultant, that have evolved as training departments have shifted to performance consulting models. It is not intended to indicate a level in the organization and, therefore, might just as well refer to a trainer as it does to the chief learning officer. The term also represents any professionals in business, government, or the non-profit arena who need to outsource.

Consultants or *consulting firms* are used for simplicity to refer to all outsourcing partners. These terms are meant to include individual consultants, larger consulting firms, vendors, suppliers, and any providers of outsourced services. The term *consultant* was selected intentionally because it often connotes partner.

Insourcing, the opposite of outsourcing, is a term that has been coined by the author for this book and is defined as retaining complete responsibility for a project. The manager who insources completes the project without help from an external partner.

What the Book Is Not

This book is not intended as a comprehensive guide to teach the basic principles of training and development. Its focus is on aspects of training and development that relate to outsourcing. However, in the process of reading this book, the training manager no doubt will be exposed to many of the basic principles and practices important to running an effective training organization.

Guiding Principles

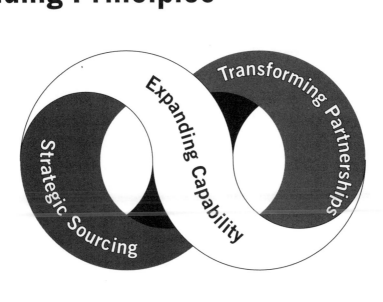

STRATEGIC SOURCING. Transforming partnerships. Expanding capability. These are the guiding principles of successful outsourcing. They serve as a compass, always pointing true north, so that even without a map, you can get where you want. If headed into unknown territory with people you do not know, it is essential to have principles to guide you. Without them, you are lost.

Strategic Sourcing

Training managers are taking a more strategic approach to their work and gaining greater credibility in their organizations. With increased change, competitive pressures, and financial demands, there is no room for a tactical approach, with training initiatives perceived as flavor of the month. Training managers must be strategic business partners, ensuring that all initiatives link to organization priorities and deliver results. Managers who outsource training initiatives are not simply coordinators of vendors and consultants. They are, in fact, overseers of both internal and external consultants and responsible for overall performance improvement efforts in their organizations. They must invest energy in activities that build a foundation for the future and yield the highest return. While tactical endeavors add value arithmetically, strategic work adds value geometrically.

Outsourcing can expand the resources of training managers and free them to operate more strategically. Outsourcing partners have a broad range of experiences and can develop the strategic capabilities of their internal partners. What is a strategic approach to outsourcing? How does it compare with operating tactically?

Balance Strategic and Tactical

Strategic leaders take a broad view. They continuously assess the environment, identify trends that impact the organization, and establish direction. They align people around priorities and help translate strategies into action. Their decisions are investments in the future and support the direction of the organization. They balance long- and short-term priorities and take into account consequences of their decisions. Examples include developing a multi-year training strategy, building sponsorship with senior leaders, and staff development.

When leaders operate tactically, their focus is short-term. They build action plans, monitor projects, and troubleshoot. Their focus is narrower with greater attention to detail. A tactical approach is required for successful execution. Examples include contracting for space, scheduling, and registration.

A balance between strategic and tactical efforts is required. A training manager may have a well-crafted strategy, but little impact if participants have difficulty registering for programs and materials never arrive for workshops.

Plan and Align

A strategic approach to outsourcing requires training managers to plan effectively and align projects and people. They anticipate future outsourcing needs and identify potential outsourcing partners. They make strategic decisions about what to outsource and what to retain. They take a long view, anticipating the impact of outsourced initiatives on the organization. They also build plans to measure results of outsourced initiatives. Finally, they apply change management principles to achieve outcomes of outsourced initiatives and anticipate risks and obstacles to project success.

When training managers align projects and people, they help others see the connection between outsourced projects and organization priorities. They work with consultants to build sponsorship and receptivity for outsourced initiatives. They also ensure alignment between consultants and internal stakeholders.

Throughout this book, you will find examples of these strategic behaviors in action. Chapter 3 focuses exclusively on a sourcing decision-making model. It will help you make wise decisions about what to outsource and what to retain, taking into account the strategic direction of your organization.

Transforming Partnerships

An organization wants to develop the strategic capabilities of its high-potential executives to help prepare them for future senior leadership roles. The training manager outsources the development of a program for these executives. In the process, the training manager learns more about strategic thinking. She interacts with senior leaders to develop the program and becomes more influential in the organization. She has difficulty confronting the consultants who falter in project management, but she learns from the experience. The consultants learn about the industry and how to make things happen in this complex organization. They are challenged by the training manager to develop a more innovative solution than they have in the past. The executives who attend the program improve their performance and have greater strategic impact. The business is transformed. The outsourcing partners are transformed.

Outsourcing partnerships are transforming. Their goals are to transform the organization. In the process, the outsourcing partners are transformed. What are transforming partnerships, and what is required of training managers to develop these partnerships? Chip Bell and Heather Shea, in their book *Dance Lessons: Six Steps to Great Partnerships in Business & Life,* define "partnership" as "*a deliberate blending of capacities for the continuous mutual benefit of involved parties*" (Bell & Shea, 1998, p. 2).

Transforming partnerships are synergistic. When both parties work together effectively, the outcome is better than either party could have achieved separately. With a high degree of trust, the partners support and treat each other with respect. They relate as equals. Each partner brings unique capabilities, neither party having all the skills required for success. In fact, it is the blending of the two that enables them to achieve better results. There is openness and flexibility, generosity of spirit, and each party learns from the other. Transforming partnerships are not conflict-free. There is a willingness to confront difficult issues, and conflict is valued as a means of strengthening the partnership and achieving better results.

Developing these partnerships is a necessity in today's world, especially when outsourcing training. Given the pace of change and the need to respond more nimbly, you cannot possibly have the resources or expertise to respond skillfully to every request for training. Even if you identify the most skillful consultants, they will need your partnership, your support and guidance, to operate effectively in your organization.

Know Your Partner

Transforming partnerships require you to spend significant time getting to know your outsourcing partners and orienting them to your organization. Find out what they see as necessary for project success. Be clear about your expectations, including the desire to have a strong partnership. Set the context for their work by explaining strategy, culture, and political issues that will help them operate more effectively. Jointly define roles, objectives, and ways of working together. Identify team strengths and weaknesses to best utilize the available talent.

Maintain Communications

Maintain a steady flow of communication. Hold regular project meetings to keep everyone informed and the project on track. Be open and ask for help as needed. Provide both positive and constructive feedback. Address conflict quickly in a way that encourages compromise and mutually beneficial solutions. Meet at regular intervals to reflect on the progress of the project and the quality of the partnership; set goals for improvement.

Respect, Trust, and Be Generous

Approach your partners with respect and a spirit of trust and generosity. Negotiate a fair contract that meets the needs of both parties. Avoid micromanaging the project and the budget. Be supportive of consulting partners with others in your organization, and help them gain access to key people in your organization. Be sensitive to other pressures your consulting partners may face. Be flexible with roles, help your partners as needed, and follow through on your commitments.

You may be wondering whether transforming partnerships are necessary on every project. In *Flawless Consulting,* Peter Block (2000) outlines three roles consultants choose: the expert, the pair-of-hands, and the collaborative roles. In the expert role, the consultant is hired to solve a particular problem with little involvement on the part of the manager. In the pair-of-hands role, the consultant is hired to implement a plan that has been defined by the manager. Here too, there is little two-way communication. It is only in the collaborative role that there is significant interaction between the consultant and the manager to jointly solve the problem. Block's description of the collaborative role closely aligns with the model of transforming partnerships described here.

There may be times when you engage a consultant as an expert or pair-of-hands. Examples include hiring a consultant to determine the technology needs of your department or engaging consultants to conduct training programs that you have already developed. Although there is no need for an extensive collaboration on these projects, a spirit of partnership is important. Help these consultants understand your organization, the background of the initiative, and the participants. They will be better able to link the initiative to strategic objectives and respond more effectively. Ask for their ideas on how to make these projects successful. Take care of logistical details, so they can concentrate on what they do best. At the end of the project, solicit their feedback to help you both learn for the future.

This book is infused with a spirit of partnership. You will find examples of ways to develop partnerships when outsourcing. The stronger your partnerships, the greater the likelihood you will meet and exceed project expectations.

Expanding Capability

Transforming partnerships require self-confidence. It takes courage to invite consultants into your organization. It is challenging to pave the way and guide them so they can be successful. It is difficult to admit to them that you may not be sure how to proceed. When conflict arises, it is not easy to address it in a way that maintains the partnership. Like any subject, the more you learn about outsourcing and practice, the more confidence and skill you will develop. How can you expand your outsourcing capabilities?

Know the Craft

The better you know the field of training and development, the better you can manage outsourced projects. If you understand adult learning theory, you will be able to evaluate its effective application to an outsourced program. If you have previously conducted a needs assessment, you will be in a better position to contribute to the questions a consultant plans to use. If you have personally developed a training program, you will be able to determine whether a learning activity presented by a consultant is the appropriate level of sophistication for your audience. To expand your capabilities, make it a priority to attend professional meetings, network with colleagues, read trade journals, and surf the Internet.

Know Your Organization

The better you know your organization, the better you can manage outsourced projects. If you understand the strategic direction of your organization, you can help your consulting partners link initiatives to priorities. If you understand the nuances of your organization's culture, you will be able to help consultants develop programs that are a cultural fit. If you have established strong networks, you and your outsourcing partners will have greater influence and be able to build sponsorship for training initiatives. The result will be improved performance.

Develop Yourself

The better you know yourself, the better you can manage outsourced projects. What are your strengths, and what are your opportunities? How can you grow as an outsourcing partner?

Build on your experiences. If you have previously outsourced projects, take time to reflect on what you learned. If you are currently outsourcing, this is another opportunity for learning. A learning journal is provided to help you capture these lessons and identify ways to enhance your future performance.

Your Learning Journal

Consider two projects, one that was successful and one that was not. Use the first page of your personal learning journal, Lessons from Past Outsourcing Experiences, shown in Exhibit 2.1, to capture what you have learned.

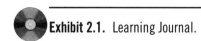

Exhibit 2.1. Learning Journal.

Lessons from Past Outsourcing Experiences

1. Reflections on a successful project

   • What contributed to the success of this project?

   • If you could repeat this project, what would you do to enhance the outcomes of the project or improve the partnership?

2. Reflections on an unsuccessful project

   • What contributed to lack of success on this project?

   • If you could repeat this project, what would you do to enhance the outcomes of the project or improve the partnership?

What contributed to the success of the project?

- Did you select a consultant who had the right expertise and was a good fit for your organization?
- Did you and your consulting partner build support for the initiative throughout all phases of the project?
- Did you establish clear outcomes?
- Did you position the consultant and yourself successfully?

What factors caused difficulties on the project that was less successful? Did you fall into typical outsourcing pitfalls?

- Did you negotiate a contract price so low that it severely limited your results?
- Did you exclude important internal stakeholders such as information technology (IT) representatives on technology-based projects?
- Did you falsely conclude that, once the consultants were hired, they could operate independently and would not require your attention?
- Did you communicate too infrequently?
- Did you avoid conflict situations?

If you are outsourcing a project now, use this as an opportunity for self-development. Complete the next page of your learning journal, Lessons from a Current Project (Exhibit 2.2). This worksheet will help you assess the quality of a current project and partnership. Invite your outsourcing partner to complete the same worksheet. Share perspectives and identify ways to improve results.

After reflecting on past outsourcing experiences, complete the next page of your Learning Journal, What Are Your Current Outsourcing Capabilities? (See Exhibit 2.3.) This assessment helps you identify your strengths and opportunities in outsourcing. As you complete the worksheet, recognize that this assessment is preliminary. You will acquire additional knowledge reading this book. At the end, you are invited to update this assessment.

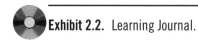

Exhibit 2.2. Learning Journal.

Lessons from a Current Project

Instructions: Consider a current outsourced project. How would you assess the project and the partnership? What is working? What is not? What, if anything, could you do to improve results? Ask your outsourcing partners to complete this worksheet. Share perspectives and identify ways to improve performance.

Name of Project _____

1. How would you rate the quality of the work that has been completed so far?

2. What opportunities are there for improvements?

3. What obstacles, if any, do you anticipate and how could these be overcome?

4. What additional work needs to be done to build support for this initiative?

5. What is your level of satisfaction with the project management?

    • Are you meeting due dates on the project plan?

Exhibit 2.2. Learning Journal *(continued)*

- Do you anticipate meeting the final deadline?

- Are you meeting budget expectations?

6. How well is the team functioning?

- Are roles and expectations clear?

- How well are team members following through on commitments?

- How satisfied are you with the quality and frequency of communication with your outsourcing partners?

- What is the degree of rapport among team members?

- How well are conflicts handled?

- How can the functioning of the team be improved?

Exhibit 2.3. Learning Journal.

What Are Your Current Outsourcing Capabilities?

Instructions: Use this assessment to help you determine your capabilities for outsourcing. Place a checkmark in the column to the right to indicate your strengths and areas for improvement. Then prioritize strengths to leverage and opportunities to improve.

	Strengths	Areas to Improve
Strategic Sourcing		
Plan effectively		
• Anticipate future outsourcing needs		
• Identify potential outsourcing partners		
• Make strategic decisions about what to outsource and what to retain		
• Anticipate the impact of outsourced initiatives on the organization		
• Build plans to measure results of outsourced initiatives		
• Apply change management principles to achieve outcomes of outsourced initiatives		
• Anticipate risks and obstacles to project success		
Align projects and people		
• Align outsourced projects to organization priorities		
• Align outsourced projects to associated initiatives		
• Link program objectives to organization strategy		
• Work with consultants to build sponsorship and receptivity to outsourced initiatives		
• Ensure alignment between consultants and internal stakeholders		
Transforming Partnerships		
Spend significant time getting to know outsourcing partners and orienting them		
• Find out what they see as necessary for project success		
• Be clear about expectations, including the desire to have a strong partnership		
• Share context including strategy, culture, political issues that will help them operate more effectively		
• Jointly define roles, objectives, and ways of working together		
• Jointly identify team strengths and weaknesses to best utilize the available talent		

Exhibit 2.3. Learning Journal *(continued)*

	Strengths	Areas to Improve
Transforming Partnerships *(continued)*		
Maintain a steady flow of communication		
• Hold regular project meetings to keep everyone informed and project on track		
• Be open and ask for help as needed		
• Provide both positive and constructive feedback		
• Address conflict quickly in a way that encourages compromise and mutually beneficial solutions		
• Meet at regular intervals to reflect on the progress of the project and the quality of the partnership; set goals for improvement		
Approach your partners with respect and a spirit of trust and generosity		
• Negotiate a fair contract that meets the needs of both parties		
• Avoid micromanaging the project and the budget		
• Be supportive of consulting partners with others in your organization		
• Help partners gain access to key people in your organization		
• Be sensitive to other pressures your consulting partners may be facing		
• Be flexible with roles, and help your partners as needed		
• Follow through on your commitments		
Expanding Capability		
Know the craft		
• Understand the principles of adult learning		
• Conduct a needs assessment		
• Design a training program		
• Develop a training program		
• Evaluate the effectiveness of a training program		
• Conduct a training program		
Know your organization		
• Articulate the strategic objectives		
• Understand the dynamics of the organization		
• Establish strong networks		
• Build sponsorship for training initiatives		
Develop yourself		
• Assess strengths and areas for development		
• Build and implement a personal development plan		
• Seek feedback to improve performance as an outsourcing partner		

Exhibit 2.3. Learning Journal *(continued)*

What are your top three strengths to build on?

1.

2.

3.

What are your top three opportunities for improvement?

1.

2.

3.

As you read this book, record your insights and continue to assess your outsourcing capabilities in the learning journal that is provided at the end of each major section. In the last chapter, you will build a personal development plan. Finally, to become a better outsourcing partner, seek feedback from current outsourcing partners. Ask the question, "What can I do to be a better partner? How can we work more effectively together?" You will not only learn more about yourself, but also will send the message that you want to be a partner. If you are not currently outsourcing projects, you can ask similar questions of internal partners. Of course, once you ask for feedback, it is important to respond and to make improvements.

Your commitment to expanding your capability is a key ingredient to becoming a better outsourcing partner. With greater knowledge and self-confidence, you can make greater contributions to outsourced projects, both in terms of the content of the work and the relationship with your external partners. As you gain broader experience as an outsourcing partner, you will also enhance your strategic capabilities. No doubt, your involvement in outsourcing will help you make a more significant contribution to your organization. You may also find that your outsourcing experiences provide some of the greatest rewards of your career.

ASTD Competency Model

Reading this chapter may have brought to mind the most recent ASTD competency model (Davis, Naughton, & Rothwell, 2004), which outlines the skills, knowledge, abilities, and behaviors required for success in the field of training and development (see Figure 2.1). The model incorporates the guiding principles upon which this book is based. On the model, note the primary workplace learning and performance roles of learning strategist and business partner and the foundational competencies of networking and partnering. These correspond to the outsourcing guiding principles of strategic sourcing and transforming partnerships. Note also the foundational

Figure 2.1. ASTD Competency Model.

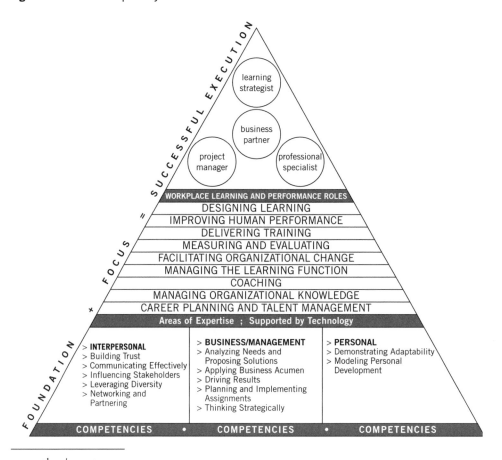

competency of modeling personal development, which corresponds to the outsourcing guiding principle of expanding capabilities.

With clarity regarding the guiding principles of outsourcing, you are ready to proceed. The next chapter will expand your strategic decision-making capability regarding sourcing. You will discover how to make wise choices about what to outsource and what to retain.

Key Ideas

Three guiding principles provide a foundation for outsourcing. These include:

- Strategic sourcing
- Transforming partnerships
- Expanding capability

Strategic sourcing requires you to:

- Plan effectively
- Align projects and people

Developing transforming partnerships requires you to:

- Spend significant time getting to know your outsourcing partners and orienting them
- Maintain a steady flow of communication
- Approach your partners with respect and a spirit of trust and generosity

Expanding capability requires you to:

- Know the craft
- Know your organization
- Develop yourself

The 2004 ASTD Competency Model reinforces these guiding principles and identifies the following roles and competencies:

- Roles
  - Learning strategist
  - Business partner

- Competencies
  - Networking and partnering
  - Modeling personal development

3

Sourcing

A Strategic Decision

Jennifer's Story

"I joined a national health care provider as vice president of leadership development. We were facing a ten-state expansion, did not have sufficient talent, and needed to improve service levels in almost every location. My department was not particularly well positioned. My predecessor had taken a 'flavor of the month' approach. I knew I needed be more strategic and support the succession planning process. I wanted to build competency models for key jobs. This work would lay the foundation for all my future programs. I also felt pressure to get a high-potential program going, since it was rare to fill a senior position internally. I knew I needed to do an assessment of future training needs. I had a number of requests for supervisory skills, time management, and presentation skills. The highest priority seemed to be presentation skills, because front-line managers did presentations in their communities regularly to generate new business. Better presentation skills could enhance the revenue picture.

"I met with my manager to confirm my direction. We agreed my first priority would be the competency study. Then I would begin work on the high-potential program and the needs assessment. I also wanted to provide the presentation skills program. It didn't seem like the highest priority, but it was an opportunity to position myself with Tom, the senior vice president of marketing, who had made the initial request. I had to figure out how to get all this work done. I knew I needed to hire consultants, but I wasn't sure which projects to outsource."

Strategic vs. Tactical Outsourcing

The decision to outsource begins with an understanding of the strategic direction of your organization. Outsourcing decisions should support the priorities of your organization and should help position you and your team as strategic business partners. Your goal should be to ensure that the organization's key priorities are addressed most fully and comprehensively. You want to apply the best resources, whether internal or external, to each initiative based on careful consideration, not gut feelings. Outsourcing is not a matter of simple task delegation.

As training manager, your goal should be to focus your energies on the most strategic activities that will yield the highest return on your investment. Beware, it is not as simple as saying you will do the strategic work and outsource the tactical. There will be instances when you have the capability to do the strategic work and will take on the initiative yourself. There may be other times in which the initiative is a strategic priority, and to get the needed quality you will outsource. The possibility also exists that you might split a project. You take on the strategic aspects, such as clarifying the need and determining the objectives, and turn the detailed development over to an outsourcing partner. You have many options.

Although there is no definitive answer regarding what to outsource, a framework for decision making that takes into account the associated tradeoffs can guide you. Seasoned professionals constantly consider tradeoffs among resources, timing, cost, and cultural implications. Viewing these considerations in the context of a sourcing decision model can increase the likelihood of effective decisions.

Strategic Sourcing Decision Model

The Sourcing Decision Model (Figure 3.1) provides a framework for determining which initiatives to outsource and which to insource. The model assumes you have done a proper needs assessment and have determined that there is a need for the initiative. Using a series of questions, the model guides you through a thought process designed to explore business priorities, factors important to sourcing decisions and associated tradeoffs.

The worksheet in Exhibit 3.1, Making Sourcing Decisions, can be used in conjunction with the model to support your decision making.

Figure 3.1. Strategic Sourcing Decision Model.

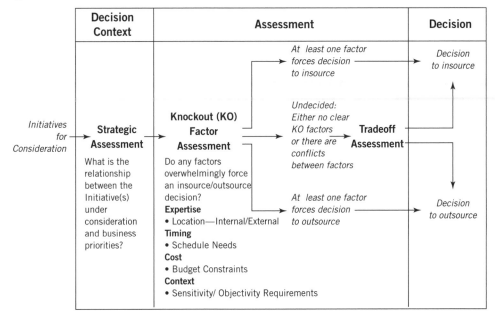

Exhibit 3.1. Making Sourcing Decisions.

Instructions: Use this worksheet and the Strategic Sourcing Decision Model to help determine whether or not to outsource. The questions will guide you through your decision.

Name of Initiative: _____

Strategic Assessment

What is the relationship between this initiative and the organization's strategic priorities?

Knockout Factor Assessment Do any factors overwhelmingly force an insource or outsource decision?	Insource or Outsource
Expertise • Does internal staff have the credibility to accomplish the initiative? • Are skills and knowledge so specialized that it requires outside resources?	
Timing • Given other priorities, can internal resources meet the deadline? • Given the deadline, do you have time to identify an appropriate external resource?	
Cost • Do you have the funds to outsource if desired? • If there is not adequate funding and you want to outsource, can you influence the appropriate leaders to obtain the funding?	
Context • Is there some cultural/political sensitivity that would require you to either outsource or insource? • Does the nature of the project require the objectivity of an external perspective?	

Exhibit 3.1. Making Sourcing Decisions *(continued)*

Tradeoff Assessment: If Conflict or No Clear Decision

	(+) Reasons Supporting Outsourcing	(–) Reasons Against Outsourcing	Implications	Decision: Insource or Outsource
Expertise				
Timing				
Cost				
Context				

The following sections present the decision model using the case study of Jennifer from the beginning of this chapter to illustrate the concept.

Strategic Impact Assessment

Begin your decision process with strategy. The question to consider at this point is:

- What is the relationship between this initiative and the organization's strategic priorities?

The answer helps you establish the context for your decision making and determine the relative importance of the initiative.

The Case Study. Jennifer needed to decide whether or not to outsource the competency project. She believed that this initiative had significant impact on the future of the organization and the future of her department. With the ten-state expansion, she knew that there would be a need for many new leaders at all levels in the organization. She felt strongly that the competencies would lay the foundation for all the work she would do in the future. She rated the strategic impact as high. Therefore, Jennifer would take the route of delivering the highest quality possible within her budget and resource constraints. She would be willing to sacrifice a lower-priority project to get the quality she needed on the competency project.

Knockout Factor Assessment

After determining the relationship of your initiative to strategic priorities, there are four factors to consider. These include expertise, timing, cost, and context. Any one or more of these factors can be a knockout factor, forcing you either to outsource or insource. Each factor has associated questions.

Expertise

- Does internal staff have the credibility to accomplish the initiative?
- Are skills and knowledge so specialized that it requires outside resources?

Timing

- Given other priorities, can internal resources meet the deadline?

- Given the deadline, do you have time to identify an appropriate external resource?

Cost

- Do you have the funds to outsource if desired?

- If there is not adequate funding and you want to outsource, can you influence the appropriate leaders to obtain the funding?

Context

- Is there some cultural/political sensitivity that would require you to either outsource or insource?

- Does the nature of the project require the objectivity of an external perspective?

The answers to one or more of the questions can force a decision. For example, if you decide that you need a program on financial planning and you do not have the expertise to develop it, then you need to outsource. Expertise is a knockout factor. The context or the nature of a project may also force a decision. For example, you might be a highly skilled facilitator but decide it is best to avoid facilitating a team meeting for the top executives of your company. You know that if you are present, there will not be the level of openness required to enhance the team's performance. The context is a knockout factor, and it is probably best to outsource. The context could also force a decision to insource. For example, you may want to engage an external consultant to provide training for a new product launch. Your culture may be extremely sensitive about competitive issues and may, therefore, be unwilling to bring in an outside resource. You will have to insource.

The Case Study. Jennifer considered expertise first. Although she had worked with competency studies in the past, she did not feel she had the expertise to develop competencies for her new organization. She believed she needed the support of an organization development firm that specialized in development of competencies. This factor seemed to be a knockout factor forcing the decision to outsource.

Wanting to do a thorough assessment, Jennifer considered the other factors. Timing seemed to lead to outsourcing. She wanted to have this work done quickly, because the competencies were the foundation of future work. Fortunately, cost was not a problem. Her budget supported the decision to go outside. Had she not had the budget, she would have faced a serious dilemma because she believed she did not have the expertise. Finally, context did not appear to be an issue. Her organization had a history of using consultants successfully. She could have been faced with a dilemma had her organization not valued consultants. Jennifer decided to outsource the initiative.

Tradeoff Assessment

There are times when sourcing decisions are not clear-cut. Either there is a conflict between two or more knockout factors, or no one factor overwhelmingly forces either an insource or outsource decision. If this occurs, you need to do further assessment.

Conflict Between Knockout Factors. What do you do if you have a conflict between two factors? For this discussion, assume that Jennifer had a conflict between two knockout factors for the competency project. She needed to outsource to acquire the expertise. However, she did not have the budget.

If caught in a similar dilemma, it is necessary to explore the tradeoffs. Examine the pluses and minuses of outsourcing for each of the knockout factors: expertise, timing, cost, and context. Jennifer's tradeoff assessment (Table 3.1) follows.

She needs to make a decision, taking into account the implications. Given the strategic nature of the project and its importance to the quality of her future work, in this situation Jennifer would probably outsource. She would ask for additional funding for the project this time, knowing she could not do so on a regular basis without damaging her credibility.

Table 3.1. Jennifer's Competency Project.

	(+) Reasons Supporting Outsourcing	(–) Reasons Against Outsourcing	Implications	Decision: Insource or Outsource
Expertise	Would get better quality solution		Creates a better foundation for future training initiatives	
Timing	Would get it faster		Gains credibility by getting results faster	
Cost		Will be over budget	May make boss unhappy; possible negative perception by asking for more funding	
Context	Mission critical		Externals elevate importance of project; they might have greater credibility with management	

Sometimes in a sourcing decision there is neither a clear knockout factor nor a conflict between factors. The situation is ambiguous with none of the factors strongly pointing toward insourcing or outsourcing. Under these circumstances, an exploration of the tradeoffs is also required.

The Case Study. Jennifer's decision about the presentation skills program provides an example. Using the questions of the sourcing decision model, this is what she understood about this initiative.

Strategic Impact Assessment

- Strategic impact was not particularly high for the presentation skills program, although stronger presentations in the community could lead to increased revenue.

- Strategic impact on the training department was not particularly high. However, there was value in satisfying the request of the senior vice president of marketing and building a partnership with him.

Knockout Factor Assessment

- *Expertise:* She had the expertise to develop training, although she had never developed a presentation skills program.

- *Timing:* There did not seem to be great pressure to deliver the program quickly.

- *Cost:* She could fund the project externally if necessary.

- *Context:* Objectivity did not seem to be an important factor, and the organization would support a program developed either internally or externally.

Jennifer explored the tradeoffs of outsourcing, examining the pluses and minuses of each of the knockout factors. (See Table 3.2.)

Based on the tradeoff assessment, Jennifer decided to outsource the development of the presentation skills program. For a reasonable fee, she was able to get a professional program developed relatively quickly. Outsourcing enabled her to focus on more strategic initiatives, and she had an early win with the senior vice president of marketing, who was pleased with the product and with her responsiveness.

You may be curious about how Jennifer dealt with the other challenges in her first year on the job. She decided to outsource the development of the high-potential program after completing the competency study. She felt that it also required the expertise and credibility of an external partner. Later that year, she started the needs assessment herself. She had expertise in this area and wanted to use it as an opportunity to build relationships with internal clients.

Table 3.2. Jennifer's Presentation Skills Program.

	(+) Reasons Supporting Outsourcing	(–) Reasons Against Outsourcing	Implications	Decision: Insource or Outsource
Expertise		Would need to do research to develop the program	Would take personal time away from other higher-priority projects	
Timing	Could deliver the program more quickly		Would satisfy SVP in marketing by delivering quick solution	
Cost	Not costly to develop; could customize off-the-shelf program		Would take funding away from other projects	
Context			Not an issue	

Your Learning Journal

The remainder of this book can help you manage outsourced projects and the relationships with your outsourcing partners to help you get the best return on your investment. Before proceeding, test the Strategic Sourcing Decision Model (Figure 3.1) and the Making Sourcing Decisions worksheet (Exhibit 3.1) on either a project you have outsourced or one you are considering. Then take a few moments to reflect on what you have learned and complete the next page of your learning journal, Sourcing Decisions: What Are Your Current Capabilities? (Exhibit 3.2).

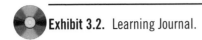

Exhibit 3.2. Learning Journal.

Sourcing Decisions: What Are Your Current Outsourcing Capabilities?

Instructions: After testing the Strategic Sourcing Decision Model (Figure 3.1) and Making Sourcing Decisions (Exhibit 3.1), use this worksheet to help you reflect on your capabilities regarding sourcing decisions.

1. To what degree have you considered the strategic objectives of your organization in sourcing decisions?

2. If you tested the Strategic Sourcing Decision Model on a past project, would you have made the same sourcing decision now as you originally made? If not, what new information did you learn by using the model?

3. What are your key takeaways from the chapter on sourcing decision making?

4. How could you improve your ability to make effective sourcing decisions?

Key Ideas

- It is important to have a strategic framework for decision making regarding outsourcing that takes into account the associated tradeoffs.

- Factors such as available resources, timing, cost, and context must be considered in any sourcing decision.

- Outsourcing decisions should support the priorities of your organization and your department and should help position you and your team as strategic business partners.

- Sourcing decisions include the following:

  - Assessment of the strategic direction of your organization and your department

  - Assessment of four critical knockout factors: expertise, timing, cost, and context

  - Exploration of tradeoffs

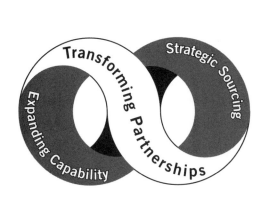

Identifying and Selecting Your Partners

PART 2 guides training managers through the early phases of an outsourced initiative, from identifying potential consultants through contracting. It begins by helping training managers develop strategies to expand their network of consultants, making it easier to find consultants when they need them. Guidance is provided for writing a formal request for proposal. The chapter on selecting consultants helps the training manager establish selection criteria and evaluate potential consultants. The last chapter explores the contracting process. Throughout Part 2 there is emphasis on the importance of building and maintaining partnerships, even in the earliest phases of a project.

4

Identifying Potential Consultants

VP, Training and Development, Fortune 500 Company

"I went to national ASTD with several trainers from my department. In the expo, we were drawn to a vendor who was demonstrating a computerized simulation. It was engaging, and we knew it could be a big hit at our company. The price tag was high, and we didn't have a current application. Three years later, when we were launching our corporate university for the top 500, we immediately thought of the simulation. A quick phone call put us in touch with the vendor."

Lesson: Even if you do not have a current need, always be on the lookout for consultants and vendors who might become future partners.

It is a challenge to identify the right consultant for a project. You may have a tight deadline and not have the time to do thorough research to find the best person for the project. The best approach is to identify potential consultants long before you need them. Not only will this approach save you time, but it will also build your knowledge of the field of training and development. This section outlines ways to identify and build partnerships with consultants who may support you in the future.

Establish Partnerships Before You Need Them

Question   **When do partnerships with consultants begin?**
Answer   **The moment you meet them.**

When you think about successes, you have had in your organization, you have probably accomplished results because of the partnerships you have established. It is rare these days that anyone achieves a goal by operating independently. Compare what it is like to make something happen in an organization when you are new to what it is like to make something happen when you have been around a long time. The simplest task can take the longest time when you are new, because you do not have contacts to help you solve your problem. Over time, if you have established strong partnerships, you are more likely to receive support when you need it. If you have helped others, they are more likely to help you. Partnerships can help you accomplish objectives more quickly.

The same is true of relationships outside your organization. It is best to establish partnerships with potential consultants before you need them. As you network and meet new consultants, assume you may want to work with them in the future. Get to know them and allow them to get to know you. Introduce yourself and explain your role. Tell them about your organization, its challenges, and current projects. Find out what kind of consulting they have done and where they have done it. What seems to be their expertise? What do they see as challenges for the future? What are trends in the field that they observe across the organizations in which they work? In all likelihood, you will learn new things from these discussions that may help you in the future. They will also learn from what you are doing. Exchange business cards and establish a contact list or card file of potential consultants.

Make networking a priority. It will serve you well. As needs for consultants surface, you will know the marketplace better and have a head start on the selection process. If they are the appropriate resources, selecting consultants you already know can pay dividends. You will be able to identify them more quickly. You will also get a faster start on your projects, having already built goodwill and trust.

Where to Look

Savvy training managers read the latest trade journals, surf the Internet, participate in local professional meetings and networking groups, maintain contact with universities, and attend conferences regularly to stay abreast of issues and changes in the field. They build their professional networks, getting to know their counterparts in other organizations and the myriad of external consultants working in the field on a local, regional, and national level.

When a need surfaces when an external partner is required, training managers who are well-networked often already have a sense of who might be a good fit for the project. If not, they can reach out to colleagues and ask for suggestions. Often their colleagues may be aware of consultants who could provide the needed services.

Professional Organizations

Joining professional organizations is important to your development. As a member, you will receive publications and associated mail that helps develop your knowledge and expertise. Meetings and conferences of training organizations are helpful places to meet consultants. Organizations such as ASTD, formerly known as the American Society for Training and Development (www.astd.org), the Organization Development Network (www.odnetwork.org), and the International Society for Performance Improvement (www.ispi.org) conduct local chapter meetings and international conferences. These meetings include informal networking time, formal presentations, and expos. Consultants often attend these meetings to market their services. Attending professional meetings is an opportunity to learn more about the field as you meet potential consulting partners.

Universities

Universities are potential outsourcing partners. Faculty members sometimes provide consulting and training services. Some universities have units dedicated to providing training services to both for-profit and not-for-profit organizations. They may have an established curriculum that is open to members of the community. Courses may include programs for senior leaders, supervisory skills, time management, project management, and various computer topics. They may also provide trainers or consultants who customize programs for a particular organization. Some universities also broker training and consulting services. They may screen consultants and provide referrals to organizations that need to hire consultants.

Networking Groups

Identify networking groups on a local and national level. These groups can be formal or informal and focus on the interests of their membership. For example, there are networking groups geared to managing the training function. Other groups focus on leadership development or technology-based training. These groups can be invaluable to you. They provide an opportunity to meet with people who have common concerns.

Director of Training, Global Communications Company

"I joined a national networking group focused on leadership development. At the annual meetings, I got to preview nationally recognized speakers and consultants. I ended up hiring several of the consultants I met through this networking group. It was a great way to identify consultants, because I had already seen them in action."

Lesson: Membership in a networking group is a good source and a low-risk means of identifying potential consultants.

Identifying Consultants for Major Technology-Based Projects

With the increasing number of organizations that are using technology-based solutions, more and more training managers are being asked to make decisions in areas in which they have limited experience. Today's training manager may be called on to make a decision regarding the purchase of enterprise-wide software, such as the purchase of a learning management system (LMS) to handle the administrative aspects of the training function.

Selection of consultants for some technology-based solutions calls for a different skill set than is typical of the average training manager. Many of today's training managers entered the field with an expertise in human resources or training. They may have held line positions in their organizations, where there was minimal exposure to technology. They typically do not have experience making major software purchases. Their counterparts in other organizations may not have made these decisions either, so they may not be in a position to refer suitable vendors.

If you are inexperienced in technology-based solutions, it is probably best to attend conferences and professional meetings where technology is discussed and where you are likely to meet consultants who could be helpful. You may also conduct research on the Internet to find experts who can guide the decision-making process in the technology arena.

Identifying Suppliers for Large-Scale Outsourcing

If you are considering outsourcing your entire training function, you will need to identify potential suppliers. Two sources will be most helpful to you: searching the Internet and trade publications. At the writing of this book, a search on the Internet brought up over two million references for outsourcing training. There are some websites dedicated solely to this topic. An excellent example is www.trainingoutsourcing.com.

As outsourcing increases in training and development, more articles are written on this subject in trade publications. These sources will help you identify vendors that handle outsourcing of training and development. They will also help you identify stories of organizations that have done large-scale outsourcing. With this information, you can identify contacts in these organizations who can provide guidance as you make your outsourcing decisions.

A strong network of peers, consultants, and vendors puts you in the best position when you need to identify external providers. Before selecting a consultant or vendor, you may want to develop a request for proposal (RFP). Chapter 5 provides guidance on the RFP.

■   ■   ■   ■

Key Ideas

- Identify and build partnerships with consultants before you need to hire them.

- Regularly attend professional meetings and networking groups to meet potential consulting partners.

- Obtain referrals from trusted colleagues.

- Make contacts at local universities to find out what training services they may provide. Get to know faculty in related fields of interest.

- Read trade journals to become familiar with trends and potential consulting partners.

- Surf the Internet to identify outsourcing partners.

5

The Request for Proposal*

Consultant, Boutique Consulting Firm

"My partner and I were invited to submit a proposal for a 360 process for five hundred managers of a nationwide bank. Before sending out the RFP, Angie, the training director, contacted us to see if we would be interested in submitting a proposal. She encouraged us based on some work we had done for her previously. She also let us know the competition—several large firms with large reputations. We were flattered and decided to submit a proposal. We scheduled a follow-up appointment to so some data gathering.

"Several weeks went by after we submitted our proposal. Angie contacted us to let us know there had been a delay in the project. About a month later, we went to the bank headquarters to present our proposal and meet with key executives. It was a good meeting, and we were encouraged.

*Special thanks to Russell Sullivan, J.D., who co-authored this section.

"Angie called us two weeks later to tell us we had not won the business. She explained that the decision had been made based on scalability and technology. She thought we would have been great coaches, but did not feel we had the technological capability to handle the project. We were disappointed, but we still felt positive about the experience. Angie had been a true partner. She kept us informed, openly shared information that would be helpful, and contacted us personally to explain the rejection."

Lesson: Partnerships begin in the early stages of a project, long before a contract is signed. Respect potential consulting partners by maintaining regular communications and openly sharing information during the selection process. Contact them to let them know your final decision. They will appreciate the respect you show and will be likely to respond and support you in the future.

The Purpose

The process of selecting external consultants often begins with an RFP. This written document specifies the services that your organization is seeking, outlines the requirements for selection, and invites potential consultants to submit bids on those services. An organization usually develops and utilizes an RFP when it is seeking competing bids for a project.

In theory and in practice, you should find the RFP process beneficial. For one, writing the RFP will help you bring greater clarity to your initiative. As a result, some training managers develop an RFP, even if they do not intend to outsource a particular initiative. If you do plan to outsource and have several consulting firms submit proposals, you will get multiple ideas for how to approach the project. The RFP also brings greater consistency to your selection process. With an RFP, each firm that bids on your project has the same starting point, making the comparison of their proposals much easier for you. Your potential consultants will also find the document valuable. It helps them understand your goals and expectations and enables them to determine whether or not they would like to bid on your project.

Not every project requires an RFP. You may have a particular project in mind and know the consultant you would like to hire. Or you may be working on a project with a consultant and decide that you would like this consultant to continue to work with you on another project. In these cases, you may actually work in partnership with the consultant to clarify the project and skip the RFP process entirely.

If you need to write an RFP, then this chapter should be helpful. It outlines the elements of an RFP, gives you tips on writing a high-quality RFP, and provides you with a sample. The chapter ends with tips on how to build the partnership throughout the RFP process.

Check to see whether your organization requires the use of a certain template for an RFP. If this is the case, use that template and refer to this section for ideas to enhance your document. Also, it is a good idea to consult legal counsel to be sure you are following your organization's legal guidelines.

A Word of Caution

One of the benefits of the RFP process is that you receive several proposals. These will help you expand your thinking about how to approach your issue. Some training managers have used the RFP process with no intention of ever hiring a consultant. They want to get ideas, but plan to do the project internally. This approach takes advantage of consultants, who generally have to put significant time and effort into the development of their proposals.

Do not use the RFP merely to get some free advice from unsuspecting consultants. This shortsighted practice could damage future partnerships. If consultants feel you are doing this, they may be unwilling to submit proposals to you in the future when you really need their assistance. If you just need a sounding board for ideas, a more ethical approach is to hire a consultant for a day or two to help you analyze your problem and determine potential solutions. You may be surprised to find that, if you hire a consultant as a sounding board, the consultant may give you time gratis, hoping that it will build the partnership and lead to future work. This kind of generosity of spirit is a quality that helps build your consulting partnerships.

Elements of the RFP

The following elements are typically included in an RFP. Guidance is provided for writing each section. The intent is to help you begin to build the partnership in this early stage of the project. The information provided is not intended in any way to provide legal advice or counsel. Exhibit 5.1 is a sample RFP.

Exhibit 5.1. Sample Request for Proposal.

THIS REQUEST FOR PROPOSAL (RFP) CONSTITUTES THE CONFIDENTIAL AND PROPRIETARY INFORMATION OF WILLIAMS INTERNATIONAL COMPANY (WIC) AND MAY NOT, IN WHOLE OR IN PART, BE COPIED, REPRODUCED, OR OTHERWISE USED IN ANY MANNER WHATSOEVER WITHOUT THE PRIOR EXPRESS WRITTEN PERMISSION OF WIC. ALL INFORMATION PROVIDED HEREIN IS PROPRIETARY TO WIC AND IS TO BE USED ONLY BY YOUR COMPANY IN ITS RESPONSE HERETO. ANY OTHER USE OR COMMUNICATION OF THIS INFORMATION IS STRICTLY PROHIBITED.

1. Introduction

This request for proposal (RFP) is issued by Williams International Company (WIC). WIC is seeking a consulting firm that specializes in organizational change and leadership development to provide its top 250 leaders with an executive development program to support the integration of its two newly merged consumer electronics retailers.

---

2. Company Overview

WIC retails consumer electronics, home-office products, entertainment software, and related services. It operates retail stores and/or commercial websites
under the brand name HighTechHut, as well as an outlet store online. The
company's 750 nationwide stores offer video products that include televisions,
digital cameras, DVD players, digital camcorders, and digital broadcast satellite systems; audio components and mobile electronics; home products con-
sisting of desktop and notebook computers and related peripheral equipment,
telephones, cellular telephones, and MP3 players; entertainment software
products, including DVD movies, video game hardware and software, com-
pact discs, and computer software; and appliances, such as vacuums, small
electronics, and housewares.

WIC is acquiring Manfried Entertainment Group, Inc. (MEG). MEG is a
specialty consumer electronics retailer that provides audio and video solutions
for the home and mobile environment across the U.S. The company sells
video, entertainment, and electronics products through a chain of retail stores.
It provides a selection of home and mobile audio and video products, including plasma and liquid crystal display televisions, digital versatile disk players
and recorders, surround sound systems, audio components, digital video satellite systems, satellite radios, personal video recorders, and digital camcorders.
It also offers home and mobile stereo installation services, as well as warranty
and non-warranty repair services. The company's in-home installation business provides design, installation, and educational services in connection with
new construction and home renovations, as well as for existing homes. Its
products include home theatre systems, satellite television, Internet access systems, and touch screen controls. The company operates 120 stores.

The merger is expected to be finalized in January 2007. With the goal of
a quick integration, the newly merged organization expects to use the business models, systems, processes, and procedures that are currently in place in
WIC. It is anticipated that, in the integration process, much can be learned

Exhibit 5.1. Sample Request for Proposal *(continued)*

from approaches at MEG. As appropriate, best practices from MEC will be implemented at a later date.

3. Project Overview

Background. The success of this merger is based on the ability of WIC to quickly integrate the two entities. Senior leaders will need to understand the direction of the new organization, their roles and responsibilities, and what it will take from a leadership perspective to make the merger successful.

In the last three years, there has been significant effort on the part of WIC to communicate the priorities of the organization to all levels of the organization. Employee engagement scores and employee turnover in that same period have improved by 10 percent. Sales have grown by 3 percent. However, customer service scores based on a mystery shopping program are disappointing.

At MEG sales have declined by 7 percent in the last three years. Rumors of the sale of the company over the last two years have had impact on employee morale and turnover. Employee opinion survey results have declined in that same period, and employee turnover has increased by 25 percent.

Once the merger is complete, it will be important for the company to operate with one voice to the customer. All retail outlets will operate under one nameplate, HighTechHut. Advertising will be consistent in all markets. Customer service, business practices, and systems must be consistent in all locations.

Project Description. WIC seeks an executive development program to help launch the new company. We are interested in receiving proposals that include a methodology (needs assessment) and design that would lead to a multiple-day intensive leadership development program. This program is tentatively scheduled for the week of April 2, 2007, in a location to be determined.

Exhibit 5.1. Sample Request for Proposal *(continued)*

Primary Objectives. As a result of this leadership development initiative, executives will be able to lead effectively in the newly merged organization including:

- Lead organizational change
- Manage a business of larger scope in a larger organization
- Integrate new team members and build high performance work teams
- Demonstrate resilience in a rapidly changing environment

The vendor will not be responsible for handling any logistics of the meeting (e.g., airfare, hotel, ground transportation, food, etc.). WIC will be responsible for securing the venue, as well as the meeting logistics.

Related Initiatives. The training organization of WIC is currently conducting a merger-related needs assessment related to on-boarding and development of job-specific skills for all employees of the company.

4. Target Audience

Participants of this program will represent all functional areas and will include all senior vice presidents and above of the newly merged organization.

5. Project Timeline

This leadership program is currently scheduled for the week of April 2, 2007. The results of the needs assessment and a preliminary design should be presented by October 3, 2006. A finalized design is due November 7, 2006.

6. Proposal Contents

Please include the following in your proposal:

a. Outline of your proposed methodology (needs assessment) and program design that best addresses the objectives of the requested program

---

Exhibit 5.1. Sample Request for Proposal *(continued)*

    b. Description of your company's capability and any previous experience in this area, specifically in the techniques to be used in this project

    c. Resumes/biographies of all consultants who will be involved in the project

    d. Project timeline and deliverables

    e. Costs, including direct service costs, speaker fees, materials, travel, etc.

    f. Minimum of three references of a similar type project including the following information:

- Company name

- Company address

- Contact name and title

- Contact telephone number

- Date contract began

- Scope of services provided

7. Proposal Format

Please provide five hard copies of your proposal addressing all items listed in Section 6 to Ms. Nancy Green by Monday, June 5th.

Selected providers will be invited to WIC to present their proposals the week of June 12th or 19th.

Exhibit 5.1. Sample Request for Proposal *(continued)*

8. RFP Timetable and Submission Requirements

The complete proposal must be received by WIC by Monday, June 5th. Mail to:

Williams International Company

Attn: Ms. Nancy Green

750 Summer Street

Maineville, Ohio 45656

An award in response to this RFP is expected by July 10, 2006. However, this time is subject to change at WIC's sole discretion.

Inquiries on all matters during the RFP process should be directed to Nancy Green at ngreen@wic.com.

Additional information

- Proposals submitted to WIC automatically become the property of WIC and will not be returned.

- To assure fairness to all participating contractors, responses received after the submission date will not be considered.

- WIC will not discuss the project budget with any prospective contractor. This will be addressed with the prospective contractors after evaluations of all proposals and any subsequent revisions have been completed.

A Statement of Confidentiality

Most RFPs begin with a statement of confidentiality. This statement often appears on the cover page of the RFP. It is best for you to seek legal counsel on the exact wording of your confidentiality statement. The heart of the statement should protect your organization, mandating that the consultant use the information and data obtained during the RFP process only for the limited purposes provided (i.e., to prepare and submit a bid for the project at hand). Often the statement will also include some similar protection for the consultant, requiring you to keep confidential the information that the consultant provides during the process.

Description of Your Organization

This section provides you with an opportunity to describe your organization to your potential consultants. You can include information such as your mission, your products and services, your parent corporation or subsidiaries, your locations, and your number of employees.

Project Overview

Try to be as comprehensive as you can in your description of the project. This will help your potential partners develop solutions that more closely meet your needs. In this section, you may provide information such as:

- Background of the project and its relationship to the organization's strategic objectives

- Explanation of the need and associated needs assessment data, if it is available

- Description of the project sponsor

- Objectives of the project and measures of success

- Relationship of this project to other organizational initiatives

- Special requirements and constraints

  - Technology-based requirements (system requirements, hardware, operating systems, network and bandwidth issues, web-based or CD ROM preferences, etc.)

  - Special capabilities or background required of consultants

- Timeline for the project

If you are requesting training services as opposed to other types of consulting projects, the RFP requires much more detail in the following areas:

- Description of the target population (including numbers, job descriptions, locations, experience level, and previous training)

- Performance and learning objectives

- Statement about the preferred learning environment

- Number of days and methodology concerns, if known

- Foreign language requirements, if necessary

- Whether or not the training will be mandatory

Expectations for Proposals

In this section, you are giving the consultants advice on the content and format for their proposals. You should request that the consultant include the following information:

- Its methodology for addressing your objectives

- Previous experience relating to your project

- A description of its organization and biographies of the personnel it would assign to the project

- Anticipated timelines for the project and deliverables

- A fee estimate (in the form of an overall project fee, cost per project phase, daily/hourly rates, etc.)

- A list of references (with a similar industry/similar project emphasis)

RFP Timetable and Submission Requirements

In this section, explain the timing of the process and include dates for the following:

- Distribution of the RFP

- Deadline for questions

- Proposal due date

- Presentation of proposals to your organization

- Awarding of the contract

Describe your expectations for submission. Include:

- Whether it should be sent via email and/or hard copy

- The number of hard copies that you want

- Name and address of person to whom proposals should be submitted

How to Make Inquiries

In this section, explain how and to whom to address inquires regarding the RFP process. If your organization limits inquiries, state that and explain the rationale.

Additional Legal Guidelines

Consult legal counsel for additional information that should be included in the RFP. Although not a comprehensive list, some of the items often addressed here include:

- Ownership of proposals

- Who can submit the proposal

- Period of validity of the proposal after submission

- Issues regarding subcontracting

- Your preferred contractual provisions (and any proposed revisions that the consultant might have as to those terms)

Exhibit 5.2, Drafting the RFP, provides a worksheet to help you prepare to write an RFP.

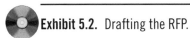

Exhibit 5.2. Drafting the RFP.

Instructions: Complete this worksheet to prepare to write the RFP. It will help you clarify the services you are seeking and outline the requirements for selection of a consulting partner.

Project: _____

Elements of the RFP	Notes

Statement of Confidentiality

Description of Your Organization

- Mission

- Products and services

- Parent corporation or subsidiaries

- Locations

- Number of employees

Project Overview

- Background

- Relationship to strategic objectives

- Project sponsor

- Project objectives

- Success measures

- Relationship to other initiatives

- Special requirements/constraints

  - Technology

  - Consultant capability

  - Foreign language needs

  - Timing

- Target population

  - Numbers

  - Job descriptions

Exhibit 5.2. Drafting the RFP *(continued)*

Elements of the RFP	Notes

- Locations
- Experience level
- Previous training
- Learning objectives
- Preferred learning environment
- Number of training days
- Methodology concerns
- If training is mandatory

Expectation for Proposals

- Methodology for addressing objectives
- Previous experience related to project
- Description of consulting organization
- Biographies of personnel who would be assigned to project
- Anticipated timelines
- Fee estimate
- References

RFP Timetable/Submission Requirements

- Distribution of RFP
- Deadline for questions
- Proposal due date
- Presentation of proposals
- Awarding of contract

Exhibit 5.2. Drafting the RFP *(continued)*

Elements of the RFP	Notes

Expectations for Submission

- How to submit (email/hard copy)
- Number of hard copies
- Name/address to whom proposal should be submitted

How to Make Inquiries

- How
- To whom
- Explain any limitations

Additional Legal Guidelines

- Ownership of proposals
- Who can submit proposal
- Period of validity of proposal after submission
- Issues regarding subcontracting
- Preferred contractual provisions

The Reverse Auction

Due to pressure to take costs out of organizations, a trend is developing in which the RFP process and consultant selection decisions are being made through the purchasing department using a reverse auctioning process. Some organizations require such a process.

In reverse auctioning, an organization outlines its needs with respect to a project and requests bids online. The bidding process is visible to all bidders and is open for a certain period of time. This is a very challenging and risky process for the field of training and development. The success of training initiatives is highly dependent on human interaction. If your organization requires you to use a reverse auctioning process, try to have direct contact with potential providers so that you get a strong sense of the services that each will provide. The direct contact with consultants who submit proposals will also help them tailor their proposals to meet your needs.

Establishing the Partnership in the RFP Process

Building the partnership is an important consideration in the RFP stage of the project. The RFP may be the first contact you have with a potential consultant. Although you may ultimately select only one consulting firm, you may eventually work with some of the "unselected" firms at some point down the line. They may also be customers of your organization.

It is possible that you may select more than one firm for an initiative. For example, you may find just the right consultant to design and facilitate a program. However, this individual may not have the expertise to conduct the program evaluation. In this instance, you should not hesitate to add a second consultant with evaluation experience to your team. Regardless of the number of consultants you ultimately select, keep in mind that the RFP phase is unique. At the same time you are trying to build partnerships with the consultants, they are participating in a competitive process. This competitive situation creates a dynamic tension in your relationships. It is therefore important for you to be particularly sensitive to consultants during the process.

Be sure to get the relationships started properly, treating all consultants with respect and providing them with the information they need to submit the best possible proposal. There are a variety of measures you can take to start building partnerships at this point.

Share Information

Although true for all phases of a project, the more information you share about your organization, your challenges, your objectives, and your requirements relating to the initiative, the better the proposals you will receive in response to your RFP. Provide as much detail as you can to those interested in submitting proposals. Make sure the RFP is clear, concise, and honest.

The RFP process may (or may not) include a follow-up conversation with each of the potential consultants after they receive the RFP. Indeed, there are some organizations that do not allow contact between the consultant and the training manager at this point. There is a fear in these organizations that there might be unfair advantage given to one firm over another. If you are in an organization like this, it becomes even more important for your RFP document to be very precise. On the other hand, if your organization allows clarifying conversations between the time the consultants receive the RFP and when they submit their proposals, you should recognize that such conversations represent a great opportunity to begin building partnerships with the consultants who are competing for the project—and who may emerge as your ultimate providers and partners.

It may surprise you to know the kind of information that training managers sometimes share in conversations to help clarify the RFP to potential consultants. Although certainly not required, some training managers let the consultants know who else is bidding on the project. Sharing this information helps consultants differentiate themselves in their proposals—and ultimately helps the training manager understand the specific benefits of working with each of the respective firms.

Sharing information about the budget is a choice point. Some training managers give the consultants a general sense of the budget they have available for the project, while others do not. There are benefits and drawbacks to both approaches. If you decide to reveal budget constraints, you help the consultants understand the resources that could be applied and how comprehensive an approach to take. Proposals will come back within your budget; however, there may be less differentiation among the solutions. By not sharing budget information in the RFP process, you may get a wider variation and potentially more creativity in the proposals. However, variation may make it more difficult to compare and evaluate the solutions. You may also get solutions that are not affordable.

Be Available

If possible, it is always best to be available to answer questions that your potential consultants may have once they have received the RFP. Some consultants will not even bid on a project if they cannot have access to someone in the organization to clarify the RFP. They feel that, without this contact, they would not be able to develop a meaningful proposal.

To show your partnership orientation, be proactive here. Follow up with a phone call to each consultant once you have sent out the RFP (assuming your organization allows this). Set up appointments to review the RFP with those consultants who are interested. This represents your opportunity to clarify the RFP more fully and respond to their questions. You may even have some ideas on the best way to approach the project—ideas that may not be evident in the RFP but that are nevertheless helpful for potential consultants to know. If a consultant is not interested in having a more in-depth conversation with you, it tells you something about that consultant. The consultant may not be willing to delve into the issues as deeply as is necessary, preferring to fall back on generic or superficial solutions. Or the consultant may simply lack genuine interest in your project. Regardless of the motive, you should take heed when the consultant expresses any reluctance to engage in such a clarifying conversation.

In your follow-up phone calls with consultants, be as open as possible and pay attention to how the relationship feels. This is actually the beginning of the selection process and the evolving partnership. What kinds of questions do they ask you? Do they dig deeply to get to the underlying causes of your problem? Do they handle themselves professionally? How comfortable do you feel? Do they seem like people who would add value? Would they be willing to collaborate with you? Would you be comfortable working with them? It may be too soon to tell with certainty, but you should at least begin getting a sense of what it would be like to work in partnership with them.

Do Not Limit the Solution

In the process of providing information (either in the written document or in the follow-up conversations), avoid limiting the potential solutions. Try not to be so prescriptive in your RFP that you leave no room for your consultants to add creative value to the initiative. Even the most straightforward project can benefit from input from others. Consultants often feel underutilized, as if they have been hired to be an extra pair of hands. There may be projects where this is necessary. However, if at all possible, do not over-control the project. Allow for consultant input and creativity. With greater openness and flexibility, you will have a greater chance for ultimate success.

Using an RFP can bring clarity to your initiative, while helping to identify potential outsourcing partners. After you complete the RFP process, the next phase is selecting the appropriate consultant. In Chapter 6, you will learn how to establish selection criteria and evaluate potential outsourcing partners.

Key Ideas

- Maintain regular communications and openly share information during the RFP process. Be available for questions.

- Do not use the RFP process as a means of gathering potential solutions when you plan to do the work without the help of external consultants. Instead, hire a consultant to brainstorm potential solutions.

- Be as precise as possible in your RFP.

- If a reverse auction is required, try to have direct contact with the consultants who are bidding so you get to know them in advance of the project.

- Avoid being so prescriptive in the RFP that there is little room for innovation and for the consultant to add value.

- At the end of the process, as a courtesy and with an eye toward future projects, contact the firms that did not win the business and explain why they were not selected.

6

Selecting Consultants

Training Manager, North American Transportation Company

"I attended a professional meeting where a consultant gave a presentation on negotiating skills. He had also written a book. I sat next to him at dinner and was very impressed. Since negotiating is critical to our business, I asked him to do some training at my company.

"Coincidentally, this consultant was considering developing an e-learning program that would teach the contents of his book on negotiating skills. We saw an opportunity to collaborate. Our company could fund the project at a substantially reduced cost. We would be willing to let him market the program to non-competing firms. We would get the training for our employees and be able to deliver it by computer. No need to pay travel expenses. Since our employees were geographically dispersed, this was a great benefit. I felt confident developing this program, because I had outsourced the development of e-learning in the past.

"We paid a significant amount of the contract price up-front to launch the project. This covered the design of the program and a prototype. The consultant identified a top e-learning firm and had a member of his team oversee the development.

"I was shocked when I reviewed the initial design and prototype. It was as if the book was put on computer. There were very few exercises, and these were not particularly engaging. I could have accomplished the same objective by purchasing books for our employees.

"By the time I reviewed the project, much of the budget had been exhausted. The consultant did not have funds for a redesign. The e-learning firm did not feel responsible, because they delivered according to the contract they had established with the consultant.

"We had numerous heated conversations to try to resolve the issue. Ultimately we abandoned the project. Looking back, I realize I signed a contract with a consultant who was a content expert, not an instructional design expert. I lost control, because I had no contact with the e-learning firm."

Lesson: The selection of consultant is critical to achieving your outcomes. Your consultant must have the required expertise for the project.

When you outsource training, you put yourself on the line. Significant funds are at stake, as is your reputation. With so much at risk, you must make wise choices. One of the most important decisions you will make is the selection of a consultant.

There are many considerations in selecting consultants, and there are even more consultants available to you. How will you decide who is the best match for your project and your organization? What approach will deliver the results you are seeking? The choices can be overwhelming and can mean the difference between success and failure on a project.

This chapter is designed to support you in selecting the best consultant based on your needs. The process outlined can help you make the proper choice and increase your likelihood of project success.

Establishing Selection Criteria

A 2003 study of human resource executives in U.S. corporations by TrainingOutsourcing.com concluded that the most important factor in choosing a training outsourcing partner was talent level of supplier's staff, over industry experience and cost (Harward, 2003). Not only do consultants need the expertise you seek, but they also need to be people you can work with effectively. There are many considerations in the selection process.

Depending on your project and your organization, you may use either a formal or an informal process for selecting your consultants. You may obtain proposals for a potential project from a number of consultants or vendors and have a variety of proposals to review. These proposals may be in response to a formal Request for Proposal (RFP) you have provided. On the other hand, you may have a general sense of the direction you would like to go, skip the RFP process and interview several consultants. There are also times when you know exactly which consultants you wish to hire.

Regardless of the approach, formal or informal, it is important to establish selection criteria that will guide your decision about which consultants or vendors to hire. The criteria will vary depending on the project. What criteria will be most important for your particular initiative? Consider:

- Expertise
- Pricing
- Approach
- Resources
- Customer orientation
- Cultural fit
- Chemistry
- Spirit of generosity

Consultants may not be able to meet all of your criteria, so it is best to prioritize what is most important. As you prioritize, take into consideration what you and your team can bring to the project as well. Remember, this is a time for collaboration. You do not have to be perfect, and neither do your consultants. It is the work you do together that will ensure the success of the partnership.

The Consultant Evaluation worksheet (Exhibit 6.1) will help you in the selection process. You can tailor it to reflect your finalized list of criteria for each project in which you engage a consultant.

The following questions can be used in conjunction with this worksheet:

1. What expertise will they bring to the project?

   - Do they have a sufficient level of experience in the areas you need?

   - Have they worked in your industry previously? How important is this?

   - Are they bringing additional skills and knowledge that you do not have on your team or in your organization?

   - What skills or knowledge might be missing in their portfolio?

   - Can they help you broaden your perspective and, therefore, improve the results of your project?

   - Do they acknowledge what they can and cannot do?

   - Are they willing to talk about projects they did that did not go well?

2. How would you evaluate their pricing?

   - Does the pricing in their proposal fit within your budget?

   - How does their pricing compare to the competition for similar services?

   - If their pricing is substantially different from others, what accounts for this? Is the price higher because it is a larger firm with more overhead? Are they presenting a more comprehensive solution?

   - Do they quote a project price or daily rate?

   - If they quote a daily rate, how many days of service do they estimate? Will there be a cap on the price?

Exhibit 6.1. Consultant Evaluation.

Name of Consultant:_____

Selection Criteria	Rating 1 = Poor; 5 = Outstanding	Comments
Expertise • Do they have related experience? • Do they have skills and required knowledge? • Do they bring a broader perspective?		
Pricing • Is it priced within your budget? • How does it compare to competition? • Is it a project price? Daily rate?		
Approach • Will their approach achieve objectives? • Will their approach be accepted? • Why do they believe their solution will work?		
Resources • Who will work on the project? • Will they subcontract? • Can they meet your deadlines?		
Customer Orientation • Do they understand your organization and industry? • Do they ask good questions and listen well? • Do they seek feedback and want to learn?		

Exhibit 6.1. Consultant Evaluation *(continued)*

Selection Criteria	Rating 1 = Poor; 5 = Outstanding	Comments
Cultural Fit • Will their style be a good fit? • Do they seem politically astute? • Will they work successfully in your organization?		
Chemistry • Do you feel comfortable with them? • Do they treat you as an equal? • Are you in alignment with their philosophy? • Do they truly want to collaborate?		
Spirit of Generosity • Do they offer helpful suggestions? • Have you learned something from them? • Do they want you to be successful?		
Warranty • Do they offer a guarantee? • Do they take any part of their fee related to the outcomes achieved?		
Recommendation (please check) • Highly recommend • Recommend with reservation • Do not recommend		

3. What approach do they recommend?

    - Will their approach accomplish the stated objectives?

    - Will the approach be accepted by your organization?

    - Is the approach off-the-shelf or is it a custom solution?

    - Are you seeking a tried-and-true solution?

    - Are you seeking an innovative approach, and can they provide this?

    - Will their recommended approach achieve long-term results?

    - Why does the consultant believe their solution will work? What rationale do they offer?

4. Does the firm have the needed resources to meet your expectations?

    - Who from their firm will work on the project?

    - Will they subcontract any of the work?

    - Can they meet your time frames?

    - What if a person who is important to your project either gets sick or leaves the firm, will they still be able to meet the commitment?

    - Will you expect them to handle project management responsibilities or will you or your team do this?

5. Do they have a strong customer orientation?

    - Have they researched your organization and industry prior to your first meeting?

    - Do they understand the issues your organization is facing?

    - Do they ask good questions and listen well?

    - Do they present solutions that fit with the culture and needs of your organization, or do they present generic or predetermined solutions?

    - Do they seek feedback from you and want to learn?

    - Do they demonstrate an appropriate degree of interest, or do they appear too hungry for the business?

6. Are they a good cultural fit for your organization?

   - Will their style be a good fit with the culture of your organization?

   - Will they have credibility and be well received by others in your organization?

   - Can they speak the language of your organization?

   - Do they seem politically astute?

   - Do they understand how to make change happen?

7. What is the chemistry between you and the consultants?

   - Do you feel comfortable with them?

   - Do they treat you as an equal?

   - Will you be able to work well with them?

   - Are you in alignment with their philosophy and approach?

   - Do they seem to care about you and your organization?

   - Can they provide the degree of flexibility that you require?

   - Will they be honest with you if something is not going well?

   - Do they truly want to collaborate with you?

8. To what degree do they demonstrate a spirit of generosity?

   - Do they share ideas?

   - Did you learn something from them in your initial conversations?

   - Do they offer suggestions on how you could solve your problems?

   - Do they tell you about similar initiatives from work they have done previously?

   - Do they seem open?

   - Do they want you to be successful?

9. What is their warranty?

   - Do they offer a guarantee for their work?

   - Do they take any part of their fee related to the outcomes achieved?

If your project is technology-based, there are additional questions for your consideration. These include:

1. What is their expertise in development of technology-based programs?

   - Is their core competency instructional design, software development, or graphic design?

   - Are their skill levels sufficient in areas that are not core competencies?

   - Are they on the cutting edge of technological advancements?

   - Do their products meet your criteria for look and feel and level of sophistication?

   - Are their products engaging for the learner, offering sufficient interaction?

   - Do they understand not only how to develop a technology-based program but also how to ensure its effective implementation on your network?

   - Do they have the level of interest and sophistication required to work with your IT department, and do they understand the importance of this?

2. How does their pricing compare to the competition?

   - Do higher prices reflect greater interactivity and more graphics, and is this important?

   - Do less expensive programs have sufficient interactivity and graphics, and will they engage the learner?

   - Is video, which is more costly, critical to the content, or could you produce a less expensive product without video?

3. What process and resources will they use?

   - What is their development process, and how will you be involved?

   - What process will be used to review the work?

- What level of flexibility will there be for changes along the way?

- If the program requires changes at a later date, will someone on staff be knowledgeable about your project if the original designer has left their firm?

- What authoring language will they use, and will you have consistency with other programs in the sign-on, mastery test, tracking, and recording program completions?

4. What is their warranty?

- What will happen if bugs are found after the development is complete?

- What level of support will they provide after implementation?

- Will a help desk for troubleshooting be available to you as you operate the program?

- Is their firm stable, and will they be around in the future when you may need them?

Rehiring Consultants

As you consider whom to select for a new project, you may wonder whether it is wise to hire consultants who have done projects in your organization previously. There can be many benefits to hiring consultants that you have worked with in the past. If they have a track record with you, you have already developed a partnership. You understand their strengths and weaknesses and know the best way to work with them. They know you and your organization. This will probably save time on your projects. However, there can be a downside to working with the same consultants. You may become too dependent on them. They may not be available when you need them. You may also limit creativity by relying on the same consultants over time.

Many training managers like to contract with a small group of consulting firms. They feel they get the best of both worlds. They work with consultants who get to know their organizations well and can, therefore, be more productive more quickly. They also benefit from a diversity of perspectives.

Working with more than one firm brings newness to the organization. You may also get better service because of the long-term nature of the relationships.

Training Director, Large Energy Corporation

"When I got the news that my company was going to double in size because of an acquisition, I got nervous. I knew we would need to provide training for the integration, but I wasn't sure how to proceed. Over the years, I had worked with three consulting firms and decided to call them for advice. They each had M&A experience. I was clear with them that I didn't know if our conversations would lead to any new business.

"They were great partners. One consultant described the merger-related projects he had done. Another shared some research on the leadership implications of mergers and acquisitions. The third allowed me to review a training program that his firm had developed. I think they were hoping to get some business, but I could tell that they were willing to help even if they didn't."

Lesson: Developing strong partnerships with consultants can pay dividends. Consultants are often generous with clients and share resources that help with future projects. When asking for this support, be honest that you are looking for ideas and may not actually hire the consultant for help with the issue.

Meeting with Potential Consultants

After establishing criteria, meet with the consultants you are considering. These meetings provide an opportunity for them to present their proposals to you. Keep in mind that the partnership is already beginning at this point. Just as you are assessing the consultants, they are assessing you. You are trying to determine whether you can establish a strong partnership with them. They are trying to determine whether they can establish a strong partnership with you. Sometimes consultants walk away from business, because they do not feel there is a good match with the potential client. Even if you do not select a particular consultant for a project, that person may be someone you would consider in the future.

Demonstrate That You Value Partnerships

Throughout the selection process, demonstrate through your words and actions that collaboration is important to you. There are many ways to signal a desire to collaborate.

1. *Build trust.* When you invite consultants to present their proposals, be as open as you can. Describe the format for your meetings and who will participate. During the meetings, explain the selection process you will use. Share your criteria. Encourage the consultants to ask questions. Reveal as much information as you can, sharing concerns you may have. Ask questions about the proposals, so that you clearly understand the recommendations. Explain your timing for making the final selection. Treat them with respect at all times, and thank them for presenting their proposals.

2. *Put them at ease.* Since consultants know they are typically competing with others, it can be uncomfortable. They are trying to collaborate at the same time they know they are competing. Try to put them at ease. Compliment them on their proposals, letting them know what you found particularly appealing. Keep the meetings professional, but as informal as possible. Have all participants introduce themselves and describe their roles. Have light refreshments available or a meal, as appropriate. Treat potential consultants as your guests.

3. *Handle the details.* Give directions to your location and make necessary security arrangements (e.g., obtaining security passes). Explain the dress code, so they feel comfortable and fit in when they arrive. Even though travel is usually the consultant's expense until the sale is made, clarify who will pay travel expenses. Make arrangements for equipment they may need for their presentations. Ask how you can make their visit go more smoothly.

4. *Honor them.* Stay in touch with consultants throughout the selection process, especially if there are delays. Let them know as soon as possible whether or not they have won the business. If they are rejected, explain why. They will appreciate your candor, and it will help them learn for the future.

Conducting the Meetings

Some training managers prefer to set up meetings with each of the consultants in two- or three-hour blocks of time over a period of one to two days. It is not always possible to do this from a scheduling standpoint. If you can, it enables you to focus on the decision in a relatively short period of time.

Depending on the importance of the project, it is helpful to include others from your organization. By involving others, you can broaden your perspective, build support for the project, and minimize your personal risk. Invite people who can help you make the best decision and whose support you need. Consider the following people:

- Your supervisor
- Members of your team who will ultimately work on the project
- Line managers who will receive the consulting services or final product
- Trusted colleagues
- Members of your IT department, if the program is technology-based

It is especially important to include representatives from your IT department if it is a technology-based initiative. When implementing technology-based programs, you are really delivering software. The IT department can help you decide whether the provider has the technical capabilities to meet your needs. By being present at this early stage, they can help everyone understand technical requirements and can plan for the implementation.

Make sure everyone from your organization understands who will be present at the meetings and the purpose of the meetings. Members of your organization should understand the goals of the project and the selection criteria. If there is a written proposal, be sure they have copies in advance. Provide copies of the Consultant Evaluation worksheet (Exhibit 6.1) to everyone. They can use these worksheets to evaluate all the consultants and provide you with feedback.

The consultants should know who from your organization will be present and what their roles are. With this understanding, they will be in a better position to present their proposals to meet the needs of your group.

Allow sufficient time for the consultants to present their proposals and to engage in a dialogue. You can probe in detail to understand their capabilities, how they will approach the project, and whether or not you feel you will be able to work with them effectively. Consider the questions outlined above in the selection criteria section. The consultants will use this time as an opportunity to get to know you better and to learn how to work most effectively with you.

Capturing feedback from others on your team immediately after the consultants depart is especially important if you are interviewing several firms. Summarize the data from Consultant Evaluation worksheets. Having the documentation will help you do a better job of comparing firms and will minimize confusion.

Auditioning Trainers or Speakers

Training Manager, Manufacturing Company

"I needed to hire a consultant to teach time management. I invited my staff and some employees from different departments to preview a program and give me feedback on the consultant. During the audition, two of the participants began to act out. They were very extreme, far more difficult than any participant we would typically have in a program. The consultant had trouble dealing with them. I could tell he was upset when he left. He called me before I could reach him and let me know that he was not interested in the assignment."

Lesson: Create a realistic environment when auditioning trainers, so they get a sense of what is typical in your organization and so they can perform well. The partnership is beginning in the audition. Remember they are evaluating you, just as you are evaluating them. Even if you do not hire them, you and your organization's reputation are at stake.

If you plan to hire consultants to serve as trainers or to give formal presentations in your organization, it is wise to audition them. How they present themselves by phone or in a business meeting can be very different from how they present themselves in front of a large audience or in the classroom. By seeing people in action, you will make a better assessment of their capabilities as a trainer or speaker.

Before inviting trainers to audition, establish selection criteria. The worksheet, Trainer Audition Evaluation (Exhibit 6.2), and the following questions can help you determine your criteria:

- Will they fit your culture?

- Do they seem to make a quick connection with participants?

- Will they have credibility with your target audience?

- Do they seem knowledgeable?

- Do they have the appropriate level of energy?

- Can they handle difficult questions?

- If you are using their materials, are the content and approach appropriate?

- Can they customize materials to meet the needs of your organization?

- If they will need to present your training materials, do they have the flexibility to deliver materials that were developed by others?

Once you are clear about the selection criteria, invite the trainers to your organization to make a presentation or to facilitate a segment of a training program. If it is not feasible for them to travel to your location, request a copy of a videotape or DVD to view them from a previous presentation. If they are represented by a speakers' bureau, the bureau will be able to forward an example of the person presenting on video or DVD. Sometimes these presentations are available on the Internet. As another option, you might consider traveling to see them in a public program. You could also ask permission to observe them presenting at another organization. Some organizations may allow this. Others may be unwilling to do so because of issues of competition or confidentiality.

Exhibit 6.2. Trainer Audition Evaluation.

Name of Trainer: _____

Selection Criteria	Rating 1 = Poor; 5 = Outstanding	Comments
Expertise • Do they have required skills and knowledge? • Do they have the appropriate experience? • Will they have credibility with your audience? • Can they handle difficult questions?		
Content • If using their materials, is the level and approach appropriate? • Can they customize to meet the needs of your organization? • If using your materials, do they have the flexibility to deliver your content?		
Cultural Fit • Will their style be a good fit? • Do they seem politically astute? • Will they work successfully in your organization?		
Chemistry • Do they seem to connect quickly with participants? • Do they have the appropriate level of energy? • Do you feel comfortable with them? • Are you in alignment with their philosophy? • Do they truly want to collaborate?		
Recommendation (please check) • Highly recommend • Recommend with reservation • Do not recommend		

If your only option is to see them on videotape or DVD, remember that this medium has limitations. Since the camera is usually focused on the presenters, you may not get a sense of the connection the presenters are able to make with their audiences. There is often not as much warmth picked up by the camera as there is in a session delivered in real time. You are not able to see how the presenters might customize their presentations to your organization. You will, however, get a sense of their ability to customize their presentations to the organizations in which they were taped.

If you are able to arrange for the potential consultants to come to your organization to conduct training, ask them to facilitate a segment of instruction that is similar to what they will ultimately do for you. You will get the best idea of how well they will perform. In the audition, if the topic is different either in content or delivery methods from your requirements, you may not get an accurate picture. For example, if you need them to conduct highly interactive training and they present a very structured lecture, you will not get a sense of their ability to deliver what you need.

When potential consultants audition, ask other people from your organization to participate. You may choose to include members of your staff, the program sponsor, or others working on the initiative. Make sure the participants understand their roles and the selection criteria in advance of the presentations. Make sure the consultants understand who the participants are.

Recognize that this situation can be particularly stressful for potential consultants, so prepare the participants. Encourage them to act like average participants. Although it is fair to challenge and ask tough questions to see how they will respond, it is not the time to act like the most difficult participants the consultants may face in your organization.

Once auditions are complete, gather input from participants based on your established criteria. Ask all participants to rate each of the consultants using a worksheet similar to Exhibit 6.2, Trainer Audition Evaluation. The use of a common worksheet will bring consistency to your decision making. Make sure all participants recommend whether or not to hire the trainers.

Senior Trainer, International Telecommunications Company

"I invited a group of trainers to an audition to give feedback on a provocative, experientially based program. It didn't go well. I have to admit that I didn't do a good job of positioning the program, and I relied on the consultant to introduce herself to the group. She jumped right into the training without helping people understand the context. The trainers enjoyed the session but didn't see the business application. They didn't endorse the consultant.

"I should have done a better job of preparing them. The consultant should have done a better job of facilitating. My gut told me it was the right solution, so I contacted the firm and asked for a stronger facilitator. I interviewed two other consultants and was immediately impressed. I had confidence they could do the kind of debriefing I needed. Just to be sure, I checked their references."

Lesson: Carefully position consultants who are auditioning. Do not hesitate to provide feedback if the audition does not go well. The intervention may be appropriate, but the consultant may not be the best match for your organization. Explore alternatives to find the proper match.

Checking References

By now you have probably narrowed the field. You may have eliminated some of the consultants you interviewed. Perhaps you did not feel they offered the needed expertise, or you did not think you could work effectively with them. For those you are still considering, you may want to check references. Contact them and ask for the names and phone numbers of two to three clients they have worked with previously. It will probably take them a few days to get these names, because they need to check with these clients to be sure they are willing to talk with you.

Many consultants indicate that their new clients often do not bother to check references. Even if you do not feel it is necessary, checking references may give you information that will help you manage your project more effectively. For example, you may discover that the consultant is not a strong project manager. Even if you decide to hire the person, you can keep this in mind and provide additional project management support to ensure the success of the partnership. Knowing strengths and weaknesses in advance can help you avoid problems later in the project.

Before contacting the references, make a list of the questions you would like to ask. The worksheet, Checking References (Exhibit 6.3), can be a starting point.

A reference check on a potential consultant is similar to a reference check on a potential employee. It is important to understand what the person did for the previous organization and how that compares with the project you have in mind. The requirements of your project might call for different skills or capabilities, so you will want the context in which the person operated in the previous organization. Part of what you are assessing in the reference check is not only whether the person can do the task, but also what kind of partner he or she will be. Keep in mind that the person is probably providing a reference for which the project was successful. However, through careful questioning and getting specific examples, you can get a sense of strengths and weaknesses and how well the person will fit your organization and your project.

The Final Selection

It is time for the final selection. Your decision may or may not be clear-cut at this point. One of the consultants may have surfaced as the obvious front-runner, or you may still be uncertain. If the decision is not clear at this point, there is some additional analysis you can do.

Review the data from your meetings with the consultants and from the reference checks, keeping in mind the criteria you established at the beginning of the selection process. Consider the major pluses and minuses of each solution. What are the key strengths of each consultant? What is the cost of each solution, and what value will you get? In the end, you will need to decide

Exhibit 6.3. Checking References.

Name of Consultant: _____

Questions	Notes
1. What kind of work did they do for you?	
2. What results did you get?	
3. Why did you choose them?	
4. What strengths do they have?	
5. What were they like to work with?	
6. What was their willingness to collaborate on the project?	
7. What are their weaknesses?	
8. How did others in your organization feel about working with them?	
9. If I select them, what advice would you give me to help me work most effectively with them?	
10. Do you recommend them and why?	

by balancing what you believe is most important for your organization. You will probably weigh the answers to the following questions:

- What quality is required?

- What level of expertise can you afford?

- Will the firm with the more expensive solution deliver better results?

- Will the firm with the less expensive solution have the capability?

- Which approach has the greatest likelihood of success?

- Which provider has the greatest likelihood of success?

- With which consultant would you prefer to work?

If you are more quantitatively oriented, you may prefer to make your final decision using a simple assessment tool such as the Consultant Selection worksheet (Exhibit 6.4). You can list your criteria, give each factor a weighting, and then rate each consultant. A sample in which a training manager evaluated two final candidates is shown in Exhibit 6.5. The training manager selected candidate B, the candidate with the highest rating.

One of the nicest parts of the project is making the phone call to the consultant or consulting firm you have selected. Let them know as soon as possible about your selection. Consultants are trying to manage their resources. The sooner you let them know, the sooner they can allocate the necessary resources. Let them know why you have selected them. Keep in mind that you are building the partnership, and they will be pleased to hear the reason for your choice. They will also probably want details about next steps, including finalizing a contract and launching the project.

It is also a courtesy to let those you did not select know that they will not get the contract. Maintaining good relationships with them is important. You may want to work with them in the future. They have put hard work into their proposals and will want feedback about why you did not select them. It is a good learning experience for them to understand why they were not chosen. Finally, they are also trying to manage their resources, so communicating your decision frees them up to move on to other work without needing to consider how to staff your project.

Exhibit 6.4. Consultant Selection.

Instructions: This worksheet can help you make the final selection of a consultant. List the selection criteria. Rate the importance of each. Then evaluate the consultants and their solutions for each of the criteria. Multiply your rating by the weighting to arrive at a score for each of the criteria. Total the scores for each consultant. The consultant you select should have the highest score.

Criteria	Weighting 1 = Low; 10 = High Importance	Rating 1 = Poor; 5 = Excellent			Score Rating X Weighting		
		A	B	C	A	B	C
Total							

Exhibit 6.5. Sample Consultant Selection Worksheet.

Criteria	Weighting 1 = Low; 10 = High Importance	Rating 1 = Poor; 5 = Excellent			Score		
		A	B	C	A	B	C
Expertise	10	4	5		40	50	
Approach	10	4	5		40	50	
Pricing	5	3	3		15	15	
Cultural Fit	8	5	4		40	32	
Chemistry	7	4	3		28	21	
Total					163	168	

Avoiding Selection Pitfalls

Selecting the right consultant is challenging. Even the most experienced training managers can choose the wrong partners. Try to avoid common selection pitfalls.

Friends Can Cloud Judgment

Be careful if you are considering engaging a consultant who is a personal friend. Your decision-making ability may be clouded by the friendship. It is best to hire consultants who are a match based on carefully established criteria. If you hire a friend who is a consultant, make sure you will feel comfortable confronting difficult issues that may surface on the project.

Who Will Actually Do the Work?

As you screen consulting firms, be sure you confirm who will actually do the work once the contract is signed. Many training managers have been impressed by an account executive and then later disappointed by the consultant who is assigned to the project. Make sure the individual has the skills to do the job and can work effectively with you and your team.

Blinded by the Big Name

Reputation is only one aspect of decision making when selecting consultants. A consulting firm's reputation is not a guarantee of success. Training managers need to do careful analysis to determine whether or not a particular firm will be able to provide helpful solutions to solve their organizations' problems.

Trust Your Instincts

When selecting a consultant, pay close attention to your instincts. Sometimes you may pick up on something that is hard to articulate. If you are hesitant, there is probably a reason. Explore the relationship more fully before making your final selection. Also consider whether there is a diversity issue at play. Are you feeling uncomfortable because the person is not like you? Sometimes engaging someone who has another point of view could add value. However, ultimately, if you are not comfortable, do not proceed. Good chemistry is vital to a partnership.

Selection Based Solely on Price

Cost is only one factor to consider in selection of a consultant or vendor. Pricing usually reflects the service that will be provided. There is a reason why one firm charges more or less than another. Is the fee higher because it is a larger firm with more overhead or does the firm provide greater expertise? Is the fee based on reputation, and is this important on the project? Explore the pricing structure carefully when making selections. A lower fee may or may not deliver the service you require. Understand the value you will get for your investment.

Sight Unseen

Carefully screen every consultant you hire. Recommendations of others are helpful, but not sufficient. You should have direct contact with all consultants you hire so that you can evaluate their effectiveness and potential for success in your organization.

You have carefully selected the consultant you feel is the best fit for your initiative and your organization and is someone with whom you feel you can develop a strong partnership. Chapter 7 outlines the next phase of the project, the contract. The contract provides an opportunity for you to clarify your partnership more fully. The right consultant and the right partnership are key to achieving your objectives.

■ ■ ■ ■

Key Ideas

- Establish and prioritize selection criteria before reviewing potential consultants.

- Consider the following criteria:

  - Expertise

  - Pricing

- Approach

- Resources

- Customer orientation

- Cultural fit

- Chemistry

- Spirit of generosity

- Rehiring consultants can save you time since they already know your organization. Be careful not to get too dependent on any one particular consultant.

- Throughout the selection process, demonstrate to potential consultants the value you place on partnerships by:

  - Sharing information

  - Treating them with respect

  - Keeping the tone informal and putting them at ease

  - Handling the details of their visit

  - Maintaining contact and providing feedback quickly on your selection

- Involve others in the selection process.

- Audition potential trainers.

- Check references to help make the final selection and to understand ways to work effectively with the consultants you choose.

- Avoid selection pitfalls such as choosing friends, basing judgment on the account executive and not the person who will do the actual work, and making a decision solely based on price.

7

The Contract*

Director, Learning and Development, International Consumer Products Firm

"I had to cut my budget and my staff, so I began to outsource some projects. I used an RFP process and hired a consulting firm to design and deliver training for our sales executives. Because of expense pressures, I negotiated a very sharp price for the project. The consultants seemed a little uncomfortable with the pricing, but I could tell they wanted the business.

"During development, I requested a lot of changes to the content. At first this didn't seem to be a problem. When I got to the third round of changes, they were resistant. They told me the changes were unreasonable given the contract price. It got pretty tense. After numerous conversations with the lead consultant, I agreed to pay more for the program to get the result I needed."

---

*Special thanks to Russell Sullivan, J. D., who co-authored this section.

Lesson: Be reasonable as you negotiate a contract. Keep the emerging working partnership in mind throughout the process. And make sure that the price you get on the front end will allow the consultant to deliver the product or service that you need on the back end.

Inexperienced training managers often feel that they are in an adversary relationship with their consultants. They feel their goal should be to negotiate the best deal, driving the contract price down as low as possible. Savvy training managers understand that driving the contract price down too low can severely limit the services the consultants can deliver and may negatively impact project results. They realize that contracting is not a contest to determine who wins. Instead, the contract should set both parties up to win. The training manager wants to receive high-quality services that improve organizational performance. The consultants want to deliver high-quality services and are entitled to make a profit for their work. These goals are not mutually exclusive—and they should be reflected in the contract accordingly.

Many training managers indicate that, on projects for which they had outstanding relationships with their consultants, the contract did not seem to make much of a difference. In fact, they often ended up placing the contract in a drawer, never looking at it again after it was finalized. This is actually what you hope will happen unless your contract happens to specify your project plan. The contract serves as a safety net that typically only needs to be utilized during the project if major differences, disputes, or violations arise. Therefore, the better the partnership with your consultants, the less likely you will need to revisit the contract.

Why Contract with Consultants?

If you are entering into an arrangement with consultants that is extensive and involved, both in terms of time and scope, then you will probably want to negotiate a formal legal contract to structure that arrangement. But contracting is not just about legal protections and parameters. It is also an important aspect of your developing partnership. As you go through the necessary and invaluable process of working out the details of the contract with your consultants, you are actually communicating expectations for the project and the relationship with each other. Through your negotiations, you are clarifying important issues, such as the scope of work, fees, the payment schedule, and issues of ownership and confidentiality. Clear expectations are foundational to strong partnerships. The contracting process can build that base of expectations.

This chapter is not intended to provide legal guidelines regarding contracting to training managers. Instead, you should consult with legal counsel when negotiating or entering into any legal contract or agreement. The goal of this chapter is to describe the typical elements of a contract, and more importantly, to provide you with guidance on how you can continue the development of a partnership through this phase of the work.

VP, Training, Manufacturing Company

"At the time, I didn't have much experience negotiating contracts. I was working with a consultant to develop a training program on project management for systems engineers. The consultant estimated that it would take three months to develop the program. I agreed to pay one-third of the contract price each month during the development period.

"We built a project plan that included regular reviews of the program during development. I was satisfied with the objectives and overall design at the end of the first month, and I paid the invoice. At the next review, I became concerned that the content and approach was too elementary. I gave this feedback, and the consultant promised to make revisions. I paid the second invoice. When I reviewed the program again, I was still uncomfortable about the level of instruction. I didn't want to make the final payment, even though, according to the contract, I was supposed to. I wouldn't have any leverage. And I worried about what would happen after the pilot if I needed revisions.

"I decided to discuss my concerns with the consultant. He was good about it, and informally we agreed to change the payment schedule. I paid one-half of the last payment at the three-month point and held back the final payment until the final revisions were made."

Lesson: When negotiating a contract, tie the payment schedule to deliverables. This approach ensures accountability for both partners.

It is customary to pay some portion of the contract price in advance. Consultants need this money to stay afloat. It is also customary to hold back some portion of your payment until after the project is complete. Holding back payment gives you leverage to ensure a satisfactory completion of the project. There is no hard-and-fast rule regarding how much to pay in advance and how much to hold back. In the spirit of partnership, a good guideline might be to make the amount of the "hold back" payment equal to the amount of the up-front payment.

Contract Provisions

Table 7.1 lists some standard provisions that you might consider including in a contract. Some helpful hints are provided for each provision. These hints can help you in your negotiations and support you as you continue to build the partnership with your consultants.

Please note that this table provides a representative list of potential provisions. You may decide that your contract does not call for the inclusion of some of these provisions. Conversely, please note that the table is not comprehensive—and you may decide that your contract needs certain provisions that are not listed. Finally, and most importantly, this table is not meant to provide any legal advice. For such counsel when drafting and negotiating any contract or legal agreement, please consult an attorney.

Table 7.1. Contract Provisions.

Provision	What It Addresses	Helpful Hints
1. Scope of Work/Services	Services the consultant will perform	Be sure there is sufficient level of detail in terms of how, what, when, and where
2. Compensation	Fees that you will pay consultant, usually on a time and materials or fixed price basis	Try to unearth potential of scope creep or any hidden costs at the outset
3. Expenses	Travel and other out-of-pocket expenses for which you will reimburse consultant	Clearly identify what you will and will not pay for here; provide guidelines, if available
4. Payment Terms	Schedule by which you will pay consultant	Arrive at an invoice and payment schedule that will work for both parties; tie payments to deliverables
5. Intellectual Property (IP)	Ownership of materials or products that are used or provided during the project	Typically allow the consultant to retain ownership of pre-existing IP; on the other hand, be sure to get ownership of any IP that the consultant specially creates for you
6. Confidentiality	Obligation to protect any of your confidential information that consultant might receive (and vice versa)	Ensure that language is broad enough to cover any and all confidential information that consultant might receive in the course of providing service
7. Term	Length of contract	Select a duration that is reasonable under the circumstances and that does not leave either party feeling trapped in the deal
8. Termination	Your rights to terminate the contract for convenience or for material breach (and, in some cases, vice versa)	Give yourself an escape option that is reasonable under the circumstances (in light of the consultant's investment and commitment, etc.)

Table 7.1. Contract Provisions *(continued)*

Provision	What It Addresses	Helpful Hints
9. Assignment	The rights (if any) of either you or the consultant to assign rights and obligations under the contract to another person or entity	Specify that the consultant cannot do so in the absence of your prior written consent
10. Cancellation	The fees that you will pay to the consultant if you cancel or postpone scheduled training classes and the like	If the consultant insists on such a policy, only agree to one that is fair to both parties; you want to be able to cancel close to the scheduled date without paying an exorbitant cancellation fee
11. Insurance	Insurance coverage that the consultant must carry	Make sure that the consultant has insurance coverage that will cover "worst case scenario" losses (e.g., bodily harm comes to participant due to the actions of the consultant); in more extensive engagements, request that the consultant add you to their policy as an additional insured (also providing you with right to be notified in advance in the event of change or cancellation of coverage)
12. Indemnity	Consultant's obligations to defend you and make you whole in the event that you are sued due to the consultant's act or omission	Pay special attention to this provision if the consultant is going to be dealing directly with your clients or customers
13. Audit	Your right to inspect the consultant's records to ensure that you were billed properly	Request that the consultant retain such records for a three- to five-year period (and give you reasonable rights to inspect those records along the way if necessary)

Table 7.1. Contract Provisions *(continued)*

Provision	What It Addresses	Helpful Hints
14. Unforeseen Circumstances	The fact that neither party shall be in default should failure to perform be due to acts of God or other cause beyond that party's control	Make sure that this provision addresses only those highly unusual circumstances that are, in fact, beyond the control of the parties
15. Representations and Warranties	The ironclad promises that you want the consultant to make about certain subjects (that the work will be performed in a professional manner, etc.)	Secure warranties from the consultant that you believe are absolutely necessary
16. Independent Contractor Status	The consultant's status as an independent contractor, not as an employee of your organization	Clarify that the consultant, not you, has responsibility with respect to tax obligations
17. Publicity	The consultant's right (if any) to advertise you as a client	Consider handling such requests on a case-by-case basis, contingent on your prior written consent
18. Dispute Resolution	The process by which you and the consultant will address any disputes that might arise	Consider arbitration or mediation as the dispute resolution mechanism; each is typically faster and cheaper than traditional litigation
19. Governing Law	The law that will govern any dispute that might arise	Request that the law of your home state govern all disputes
20. Notice	The process by which you or the consultant will formally notify each other pursuant to any provision in the contract	Permit notice by fax, overnight delivery, or whatever is your preferred mode of written communication
21. Merger and Amendment	The fact that this contract supersedes all prior writings or conversations re: the subject matter, and the fact that you can amend at a later date if need be	Delineate that all such future amendments should be mutual and in writing

Remember, this table merely provides a general overview of potential contractual provisions. When it comes time to negotiate, draft, and sign a contract, you should consult an attorney.

Independent Consultant

"A training manager hired me to conduct six training sessions for a group of middle managers. The first three sessions went well, and I was looking forward to the remaining sessions. The training manager called me a week before the last three sessions to say that the remaining programs had to be cancelled due to shifts in business priorities. I reminded the training manager that the contract called for payment of a cancellation fee if sessions were cancelled within thirty days of the program. The training manager refused to pay. He argued that they would conduct the sessions the following year, so I would get paid then. I was angry. I had refused other business to do these training sessions. I knew there was nothing much I could do."

Lesson: As an ethical partner, follow through on all contractual obligations. If not, you will certainly get a reputation in the community as a training manager consultants will want to avoid.

Letters of Agreement

Some projects are not particularly complex and do not require a full contract. An example might include hiring a consultant to conduct one or two training sessions. If the engagement with the consultant is a limited one, then you might consider a simple one- to two-page letter of agreement that covers just the core elements. The letter of agreement might describe the services that the consultant will perform, the compensation that you will pay, and other elements that you believe to be crucial (confidentiality, intellectual property, etc.). Such a letter of agreement is usually shorter and more informal in tone and language than the formal written contract. As long as both parties sign it, however, such a letter of agreement has the same binding effect as that of a formal written contract. Letters of agreement are also sometimes used as an interim step toward a contract if you have a tight deadline.

Your Learning Journal

Part 2, Identifying and Selecting Your Partners, ends here. In this part of the book, you have explored ways to identify potential consultants, tips for writing an RFP, and ideas for how to select the right consultants and contract with them. Before proceeding to Part 3, Navigating Projects While Strengthening Partnerships, the chapters of the book that take you step-by-step through an outsourced initiative, capture what you have learned using the next page of your personal learning journal (Exhibit 7.1).

Exhibit 7.1. Learning Journal.

Identifying and Selecting Outsourcing Partners

How Can You Improve Your Outsourcing Capabilities?

Instructions: Use this learning journal to help you determine your capabilities regarding identifying and selecting outsourcing partners. The questions below will help you summarize what you have learned in Part 2 and determine ways to improve your performance.

1. How extensive is your current network of potential outsourcing partners?

2. How could you expand your network so that you have outsourcing partners available when you need them?

3. What lessons have you learned regarding writing an RFP and the RFP process that might help you in the future?

4. How can you strengthen your selection process for future outsourcing partners based on what you have learned?

5. How can you improve contracting with potential outsourcing partners based on what you have learned?

Key Ideas

- Make the contract the vehicle for clarifying important issues, such as the scope of work, fees, the payment schedule, and issues of ownership and confidentiality.

- Be reasonable and negotiate a price that reflects the partnership and enables the consultant to deliver the product you want. Negotiating too low a price may limit the solution.

- Tie the payment schedule to deliverables.

- Consider the use of a letter of agreement if the project is not particularly complex.

- Operate as an ethical partner by following through on all contract obligations.

- Always seek legal counsel when negotiating or entering into any contract or legal agreement.

Part 3

Navigating Projects While Strengthening Partnerships

PART 3 begins at the point the training manager is ready to launch an outsourced project by exploring how to properly position consultants in the organization. Positioning is followed by a discussion of planning for and conducting the project kick-off meeting. The chapter on project management helps the training manager understand the role of the project manager and how to manage scope, risk, resources, and communications. Chapters 11 through 14 focus on how to work successfully with consultants and vendors on an outsourced training initiative from the assessment phase through design, development, implementation, and evaluation. This part ends with a discussion of how to wrap up a project by evaluating the overall effectiveness of the project and the team.

Positioning Consultants in Your Organization

Vice President, Training, Energy Corporation

"I hired a consultant to develop customer service training for a call center. We arranged for her to spend two days monitoring calls, conducting focus groups with customer service reps, and interviewing managers. The consultant said that the customer service reps and their managers were friendly and enthusiastic, but she sensed they were holding back.

"I contacted the HR manager in the facility. He had set up the interviews and focus groups but had done little to prepare the organization for the needs assessment. Employees were hesitant to be open."

Lesson: Prepare your organization for consultants. Help internal clients build partnerships with consultants who will be involved on projects.

When you hire external consultants, one of your primary goals is to help make them successful. Partnership is two-way. While you are helping to make consultants successful, they are helping to make you successful. A way to contribute to their success is to position them properly in your organization with your internal clients and key stakeholders. This chapter describes the resistance that typically occurs when consultants are engaged and what you can do to increase the likelihood of their acceptance. It also speaks to the issue of how you position yourself in your organization when consultants are involved.

Consultants Seen as Threats

It is not unusual for employees in your organization to feel some level of threat when consultants are hired. You may feel some threat as well. Why is this?

In today's world of outsourcing, employees worry about whether or not their work can be outsourced. Their concerns are sometimes accurate, and the presence of a consultant may signal additional outsourcing. A consultant is also a sign of change. People in your organization may fear the unknown and prefer to maintain the status quo. Introducing an expert, even for a small project, might make some people feel concerned that their skills are unsatisfactory. They fear exposure. They may think that, if they had the capabilities, there would be no need for a consultant. Consultants may have worked in the organization in the past, and there may have been no appreciable difference as a result of their involvement. Sometimes administrative support staff worries that the addition of a consultant will increase workload.

Be aware of your own feelings about using consultants before attempting to deal with those of others. Are you enthusiastic about working with consultants? Do you see the benefits to you and your organization? Are your insecurities stirred up? Are you feeling competitive? Are you worried that you may not look as good to your organization because the consultants have expertise that you do not have? These feelings are typical when you begin to work with consultants.

Monitor the feelings of threat, because they may impact the project and your partnership. If threatened, you may unintentionally set consultants up to fail. An example might be reluctance on your part to give the consultants the access they need to key people in your organization. You might be less willing to try innovative approaches. If there are difficulties on the project, you may find yourself blaming the consultants so you look better in the organization.

To help with these issues, consider reframing the situation. Consultants can be an excellent support. They can help you with problems you might not have been able to solve independently. Since they may have different expertise, you have the opportunity to learn from them. Their success is built on your success, so they are probably committed to helping you succeed. In a world of constant change, a different set of eyes and ears may help you implement new initiatives. Giving them access to people in your organization may actually be more of a benefit than a threat. Finally, recognize that it takes self-confidence to work with consultants.

If clear about your own feelings, you will be more able to deal effectively with the feelings of others. Keep in mind that the concerns mentioned are legitimate and may lead to resistance. Depending on the degree of threat, you may find some employees react by being uncooperative. They may not follow through on commitments. They may not show up to meetings or may arrive late. They may withhold information that consultants need. Resistance may impede progress. You cannot eliminate all resistance. However, you can introduce consultants to your organization in a way that creates the least threat, builds receptivity, and paves the way for the greatest partnership.

Who to Involve

Before launching a project, determine who needs to be informed about the project and who should meet the consultants. Consider the following:

- Who initiated the project?
- Who is the internal client?
- Who are the key sponsors?
- Who will be involved?

- Who needs to support the project for it to be successful?

- Who will the project impact?

The answers to these questions will help you generate a list of stakeholders who need to know about the project and the consultants who are involved. As you can see by the list of questions, you are thinking not only about who to involve but also about issues of support. Consultants can help you with these issues. By discussing the players with your consultants, they will better understand the climate and political issues. They can help you strategize ways to build better support. Exhibit 8.1, Who Needs to Be Involved to Ensure Project Success?, is a planning tool for this purpose.

The individual who has initiated the project can make a big difference regarding the support the project receives. Projects initiated by a line manager or senior executive typically have more legitimacy. They may get more attention simply because they have senior management sponsorship. However, it is still important for you to continue to build support. Just talk to senior leaders about what it takes to get employee support for a change. You will end up talking to a group of people who often feel frustrated by how long it takes to get employees on board and moving forward together. Just because a senior leader says something, it does not make it so. If you are the initiator of the project, you will need to identify sponsors in the organization and work with them to build needed support.

If your project is technology-based, be sure to get your IT department involved early and often. You want to be sure that your project fits with their priorities and that they help you with the technical specifications. You might have an e-learning consultant produce an award-winning program that never is implemented because your IT department was not on board. Many a computer or web-based project has failed because there was insufficient IT support for the project. Do not minimize the importance of IT support.

Exhibit 8.1. Who Needs to Be Involved to Ensure Project Success?

Instructions: This worksheet is a planning tool. It can help you determine who needs to be involved in your organization to help make your project successful. Consider your key stakeholders for the initiative. What level of support/sponsorship do you currently have? What is needed? How can you build greater support/sponsorship?

Project: _____

Key Stakeholders	Current Degree of Support	Ways to Improve Support
1.		
2.		
3.		
4.		
5.		
6.		
7.		
8.		
9.		
10.		
11.		
12.		

How to Explain the Project to Employees

CLO, Pharmaceutical Company

"Our company was going through a major reorganization. We sold senior management on the value of providing training on change management to support the reorganization. We needed to do a lot of training in a very short period of time, so I hired two consultants. I wanted each member of my team to co-facilitate with an external consultant. I could sense my staff were nervous. They were worried about not looking as good as the outside experts. I had to be very careful about how I introduced the project to them. I talked about how much we would all learn. I also made sure my staff understood that the consultants would bring their expertise about change management, and we would bring our expertise about the culture and the political environment. It turned out to be a great partnership, and we really did learn a lot from each other."

Lesson: Be sure to position consultants appropriately in your organization. Stress the benefits to individuals and the organization, so that you can minimize the threat.

When introducing a project and the consultants who are involved to other employees in your organization, discuss the following:

- The purpose of the project
- Its link to strategic objectives
- Anticipated outcomes
- Processes that will be used, if known
- Time frames for the project
- The employees' roles in the project
- Who the consultants are
- Consultants' backgrounds
- Why consultants have been chosen

- How and when employees will interact with the consultants

- The benefits of working with the consultants

You want to build receptivity and support. As you position the project and the consultants, consider your audience. What will be important to them? Why would they want the project to be successful? What concerns will they have? After explaining the project details, ask for reactions. Solicit suggestions on how to make the project successful. Ask for support of the initiative. The worksheet, Positioning the Project and the Consultant (Exhibit 8.2), is a tool to help you prepare for your conversations.

How to Introduce Consultants

If the project is sponsored by a senior leader or a line manager, it is best for that person to introduce the consultants and announce the project to the key people who are involved. This involvement brings greater credibility. If you are the sponsor of the project, you will take on this role.

You have the choice of introducing the project and consultants by an in-person meeting, videoconference, phone call, or email. Geography and cost may dictate your choice. However, recognize that a face-to-face meeting is more likely to help develop a personal connection as compared to an impersonal email.

Examples of Ways to Introduce Consultants

There will be times when you meet jointly with consultants and stakeholders in your organization. Other times, you may have consultants meet with employees independently. Some examples follow.

Phone Ahead. You have hired a consulting firm to help you develop a computer-based training program. Although you have done an initial analysis, you have contracted with the firm to conduct a more detailed needs assessment. You have identified several subject-matter experts for the consultants to interview. You phoned each of them in advance, introduced the project and their roles, and explained about the consultants and their roles. You explained that the consultants would contact them shortly to arrange a meeting time.

Exhibit 8.2. Positioning the Project and the Consultants.

Instructions: This worksheet is a planning tool. It can help you plan conversations in which you introduce projects and consultants to your organization. Your objective is to build receptivity for the project and the consultant. Think through the topics listed below. When meeting with key stakeholders, make sure you have a dialogue. Your goal is not only to educate them but also to learn how you can make the initiative more successful.

Project: _____

Topic	Notes
Purpose of the project	
Anticipated outcomes	
Processes that will be used	
Timing	
Who the consultants are	
Consultants' backgrounds	
Why consultants were chosen/ benefits of working with them	
How and when employees will interact with consultants	
Person's role	
Ask for reactions to the project	
What barriers are evident?	
Suggestions to make the project more successful	
Ask for support of the initiative	

Joint Meeting. You have hired a consultant to help evaluate the effectiveness of a leadership program. You want your supervisor's support for this project because you believe that you should do more evaluation work in the future. You also feel that you are not an expert, and the consultant can do a better job of helping your supervisor understand the key issues in an evaluation project. You have explained the project to your supervisor, told him about the consultant, and obtained his commitment to meet with both of you. In the meeting your supervisor asks questions you are unable to answer, so you are glad you have arranged a joint meeting. It has been a good learning experience for both of you.

Advisory Board. You are developing a large computerized simulation that models your entire organization. The firm you have hired wants to interview representatives from all major business functions to be sure that the product they develop is realistic and reflects the future direction of your company. Since this is the first time you have initiated a project of this magnitude, you know that project support is critical. You decide to form an advisory board with a representative of each business function. You invite each member of the advisory board to a centrally located meeting to review the project objectives and meet with the consultants. Your plan for the meeting includes break-out sessions in which you ask members of the advisory board to provide input on the simulation design. Although you know that the consultants will need to follow up with each member of the advisory board to obtain more information, you feel this approach has many benefits. These include:

- Saving you time from needing to explain the project to each member of the advisory board individually

- Encouraging discussion about the business and the project among members of your advisory board, which may lead to more creative solutions

- Introducing your consultants to your organization and helping them to see your organization in action

- Helping your consultants build partnerships with the advisory board

Helping Consultants Connect with Senior Leaders

Vice President, Corporate University, Paper Products Company

"Our program for high potentials focuses on strategic thinking. I brought in a strategy expert from a well-respected university to kick off the training. He would spend one day working with our high potentials. The following day, the CEO would talk about how strategic decisions were made at our company. I wanted it to be a seamless experience for participants, so I knew I needed to get my CEO and the strategy expert together. I set up a meeting for the three of us in which we reviewed the objectives of the program and the content. I always find these meetings personally enriching. Plus, I think it helps position our department."

Lesson: As appropriate, give consultants access to key people in your organization.

You may want to help consultants interact with key people in your organization for a variety of reasons including:

- Needs assessment

- Preparation for a program

- Evaluating the effectiveness of a program

Consultants often want to connect with senior leadership. You have a choice, either to help pave the way or not. The consultant may want to meet senior leaders for the following reasons:

- To build support for a project

- To develop a greater understanding of the issues

- To develop additional business

It can be very helpful for you to have your consultants meet with your senior leadership. You will need to assess how important this contact is to the success of your project. The size of your organization, the amount of time you typically can get with your senior leaders, and the importance of the project will dictate whether or not you choose to introduce the consultants to senior leaders. As mentioned previously, be aware of your feelings in this matter. If you decide not to allow the contact, what is your motivation? Is the contact unnecessary, or are you too threatened to allow it to happen?

Helping Consultants Connect with Administrative Support Staff

If you have agreed to provide administrative support to consultants, it is important for this aspect of a project to run smoothly. Many consultants indicate that they do not receive the administrative support they were promised. Examples are administrative assistants who do not schedule needed appointments, phone calls not returned, training rooms not properly set up, and materials improperly duplicated or shipped. Administrative support has significant impact on the success or failure of a project. If you promise to provide administrative support, be sure to involve your administrative assistant early. Make sure the individual understands the importance of the project and the connection between the administrative details and project success. Be sure to introduce the consultants to the administrative assistant and help them to build the needed partnership.

Solicit Feedback

In the early stages of a project, it is a good idea to solicit feedback on the consultants. Follow up with people who have interacted with them. How are they perceived? Are they able to make connections in your organization quickly? Do people feel comfortable with them? Do they handle themselves professionally?

After collecting this information, provide feedback to the consultants, telling them what is working and what is not. This feedback gives them the opportunity to make adjustments.

Since you are building partnerships, it is also an opportunity for you to ask for feedback from the consultants. They have a responsibility to let you know what they are learning. The following questions may help you:

- What have they noticed about your organization, its culture, leadership, and overall effectiveness?

- What can they tell you about your organization that would be helpful for you to know?

- What kinds of issues are surfacing? How will this impact the project?

- What feedback do they have about your department?

- Are there suggestions for improvement?

- What feedback do they have about you?

- What can you do to be more helpful?

This feedback can be given informally either in person or by phone. It keeps everyone focused on delivering the best service while building a strong partnership.

Positioning Yourself

This chapter has been about positioning consultants in your organization. Before moving forward, consider how you want to position yourself in your organization. It is important for you to see yourself as a leader in performance improvement and to position yourself as such. Many consultants encourage their internal partners to take an active and visible role in initiatives. They are surprised by the ease with which training managers give up the chance to facilitate in front of senior leaders, participate in a needs assessment, or develop an internal case study.

When working with consultants, you may be worried that comparisons will be made and you might not appear as competent. There is also a risk that you are missing an opportunity to position yourself with your key stakeholders. You may limit your visibility and your opportunity for learning by remaining too far in the background if you always allow consultants to take the lead.

Step forward. Have a discussion with your consulting partners about your role. Are there certain areas in which it makes more sense for the internal to do the work? For example, if there is a discussion of organization strategy, does it make more sense for you to take the lead since you are more expert than the external? Does it make more sense for you to lead the discussion on action planning because you will be the one to support and follow up with participants? Are there areas in which you could jointly do the work? For example, could you conduct focus groups with your consulting partners or co-facilitate a segment of instruction? By taking the lead, you are likely to build greater self-confidence, improve your capability as a training professional, and enhance your credibility in the organization.

This chapter has explored the importance of properly positioning consultants in your organization so that there is receptivity to the initiative and the consultant(s) you have engaged. Now you are ready to launch the project. The chapter that follows helps you plan and conduct a comprehensive kick-off meeting so that your initiative gets off to the right start.

Key Ideas

- It is important to prepare your organization for the involvement of consultants.

- Position consultants properly in your organization to minimize the feelings of threat among employees.

- Before launching a project, determine who needs to be informed about the project and the consultants. Make sure you get them on board.

- Always be conscious of the need to build sponsorship throughout the life of your project.

- Help consultants gain access to senior leaders if this is important to the project.

- Provide the administrative support that is required for project success.

- Solicit feedback from others about the consultants early in the project. Provide this feedback to the consultants, so that they can make adjustments as needed to become more effective in your organization.

- Solicit feedback from the consultants early in the project. They can teach you about your organization.

- Carefully consider how you wish to be involved when working on projects that involve consultants. Take opportunities to position yourself with senior leaders and learn from these experiences.

9

Launching the Project

Training Manager, Specialty Store Retailer

"I hired a consulting firm to develop a technology-based selling skills and product knowledge training program. My team did a good job of marketing the program to store managers. By the time the program was ready, there was great excitement. Everyone understood that a technology-based program was the best way to deliver training to a large, geographically dispersed audience. The program looked professional. It was engaging and had significant interaction to keep associates involved. Unfortunately, we didn't do a good job of involving IT. They were difficult to work with, so we just moved forward on our own. The program launch was tough. The training program worked well. However, while associates were online for training, cash registers didn't work. Management was furious. There were lost sales while the problem was being resolved. None of us fully understood the impact of the program on the network. Eventually the issue was resolved, but not without headaches for everyone involved."

Lesson: Stakeholder involvement is fundamental to project success. Early involvement of IT is especially important on technology-based projects.

The Kick-Off Meeting

You have negotiated the contract successfully and prepared the organization. Now it is time to launch the project through a structured kick-off meeting. This meeting is a forum to say what was not said in the RFP and to establish a project roadmap. It is the opportunity for you and your consultants to get to know each other better and get the project started properly. It is a key to establishing a partnership built on openness and trust.

The kick-off meeting is a microcosm of the partnership. Peter Block comments in *Flawless Consulting,* "The personal interaction between the consultant and the client during the initial contracting is an accurate predictor of how the project itself will proceed" (Block, 2000, p. 69). Block is referring to early meetings in which the client and consultant define the project, their needs, and how they plan to work together. As you plan and conduct the kick-off meeting, be a role model for how you want the relationship to develop. Your behavior will signal the degree to which you want this project to be a collaborative effort.

Planning the Kick-Off Meeting

Taking time to plan the kick-off meeting will serve you well. Consider the logistical arrangements for the meeting, the objectives and agenda, who will attend, and roles people will play. Thorough planning will get your project started properly.

Because a primary goal for the kick-off meeting is to build a foundation for a strong partnership, involve your consultants in the planning. Set a phone appointment with them to brainstorm the goals for the kick-off meeting and topics for the agenda. They will be able to give you guidance on what is important to cover. The worksheet, Kick-Off Meeting Plan (Exhibit 9.1), is a tool you can use to plan the meeting with your consulting partners.

Exhibit 9.1. Kick-Off Meeting Plan.

Instructions: Use this worksheet with your consulting partners to help plan your kick-off meeting.

Project	
Date/Time	
Location	
Participants	
Agenda • Welcome/Introductions • Agenda Overview • Project Objectives • Context Setting • Project Planning • Roles and Responsibilities • Communications • Next Steps • Partnership Update	
Materials/Equipment	
Logistics • Hotel • Travel • Meals • Security	

Confidentiality

Even while planning for the kick-off meeting, you will begin to share information about your organization. Many organizations expect consultants to sign confidentiality agreements. If yours is an organization that expects a signed agreement, you will want the consultants to do this prior to the kick-off meeting in which you are sharing detailed information about your company, its strategic objectives, issues regarding personnel, and other confidential information. The confidentiality agreement is often signed at the same time the contract is signed and may be included in the contract. If for some reason you have not yet signed a contract that includes a confidentiality statement, you may have a separate agreement drawn up for signature.

Where to Hold the Meeting

One of your first considerations is where to hold the meeting. Although it might be more expensive, be sure to hold this meeting in person. When you are together around the planning table, it is more likely that you will be able to build rapport. You will get to know each other better than if you held a meeting by phone. Not all meetings will need to be done face-to-face. Many of your later check-in meetings can be done by phone and email.

What will you need to make the kick-off meeting successful? Consider the following:

- Quiet, comfortable location that accommodates the number of participants
- Computer and word processing for note taking
- Projection capabilities
- Flip charts or white boards
- Access to relevant information
- Easy access to food for meals
- Easy access to hotels if overnights are needed

Decide whether to hold the meeting at your location, at the consultants' office, or at a third location. Most organizations decide location based on convenience and cost of travel. Consider whether it is more expensive for you to go to the consultant or for the consultant to travel to you. Cost is usually dependent on the number of people who need to travel. Sometimes there is information that is needed for the meeting and more readily accessible at one location as compared to another. If for some reason the consultants have not yet seen your location or you have not seen theirs, this might cause you to choose one site over another. It may help the partnership if you each take at least one opportunity to host the other.

Training Manager, Consumer Electronics Company

"I've developed several computer-based training programs with outside vendors. It's complex and takes a lot of resource on the vendor side. There are programmers, graphic designers, course developers, a project manager, network experts. They work on multiple projects and do a lot of juggling.

"I made sure we held the project kick-off meeting at their place. I wanted to get to know who would be working on my program. We're not so easy to work with. Our standards are high, and we always seem to need a lot of revisions. I wanted the opportunity to build personal connections. I figured if they knew me, they might be more open to changes I requested down the line. Meeting at their place also gave me an opportunity to view samples of their other projects and let them know what I found appealing."

Lesson: Consider all the people who contribute to your projects when you hire consultants. Although you will probably only interact with a few representatives of the firm, there may be many others who contribute to the end result. If possible, take the opportunity to establish partnerships with the entire team.

Planning the Agenda

Plan your agenda carefully. What are the most critical things you want to accomplish in this meeting? Kick-off meetings typically include the following agenda items:

- Welcome and introductions
- Overview of the agenda
- Review of project objectives
- Organization issues that impact the project
- Consultant issues that impact the project
- The project plan and timing
- Key players, their roles and responsibilities
- Plans for communications
- Next steps and accountabilities
- Feedback on the effectiveness of the kick-off meeting

Remember that involving the consultants in planning the agenda signals your desire to establish a partnership. In your conversation, find out what is important to them. What do they want to accomplish? Share your goals for the meeting. Discuss who you think should attend. Determine the length of time needed for the various topics. Jointly finalize the agenda.

Logistical Arrangements

Everything you do sends a signal, even how you handle logistics. Handle the logistics with professionalism. You will send the message that quality and good customer service are important to you and your organization.

You may want to use the agenda planning phone call to clarify the logistics for the meeting, including location, travel plans such as flights, hotels, and directions to the meeting, and how expenses are to be handled. If you have an administrative assistant on staff, you may want that person to make these arrangements.

Consultant expenses for the kick-off meeting are generally reimbursable. Take this opportunity to explain your organization's travel guidelines. If these are available in print, send them to the consultants if the guidelines were not previously included as an attachment to the contract. Clarification avoids confusion. The following questions will guide your discussion:

- What does your organization expect of consultants when they travel?

- Are they expected to follow the same guidelines as employees?

- Do they need to stay in organization-approved hotels?

- Does your organization want you to make their flight and hotel reservations?

- Do they take a taxi, car service, or shuttle from the airport?

- How do they submit expenses for reimbursement?

- What documentation is required?

Clarifying how to handle these logistical aspects of the project will avoid the frustration of resubmitting expenses for reimbursement and/or delayed payments.

Let the consultants know if there are any security issues at your building. Do they need to show identification at a security desk if the meeting is held at your location? Will they need a badge to enter the building? If necessary, alert your security personnel that the consultants will be arriving. Your goal is to make the logistics go as smoothly as possible. Avoid hassles so that your meeting can start on time and energy is spent on the most important aspects of the project.

If you are hiring consultants for international assignments, there may be special requirements regarding their ability to work in a foreign country. Help research any special visas or work permits they may need. International travel is demanding. Your attention to detail in this area will help your partners have an easier time and avoid trouble at immigration check points.

Inviting the Appropriate People

Have a discussion with the consultants about who should attend the kick-off meeting. Who from your team will play an important role on the project and should, therefore, be present? Who from the consulting firm should also be present?

Not every person needs to attend the entire meeting. Is there a senior leader who is a sponsor of the project? Should that person help to explain the purpose of the project? Is it necessary for the leader to attend the entire meeting or perhaps just attend a portion of the meeting? Are there subject-matter experts who should be present? Would it be important for them to learn about the project and their roles in more detail? Should there be an opportunity for the administrative staff members to introduce themselves and clarify their roles? Most of us find it much easier to establish rapport and work with people we have met previously. The kick-off meeting provides this opportunity.

Recall the first story in this section, when there was insufficient IT involvement. If your project is technology-based, invite the appropriate IT representative to the meeting. The issue of IT involvement is a theme that you will hear over and over again when you are dealing with technology. It is never too soon to get your counterparts in IT involved. The success of a technology-based project is highly dependent on the support you receive from IT. The more they understand your project and its importance, the better the support. They also need to be fully knowledgeable about your project from the start so that they understand the implications of the project on your organization's network. They will help you explore issues of compatibility regarding hardware and software. Their participation helps to ensure success.

Whether your consultants are working on a technology-based solution or not, they will greatly appreciate your efforts to make the kick-off meeting go smoothly. A well-planned kick-off helps launch your project and your partnership.

Conducting the Kick-Off Meeting

Your meeting is planned. Now you will want to continue developing the partnership by helping participants feel comfortable, working through the agenda in a collaborative way, sharing as much information as possible, establishing clear expectations, and ending the meeting by asking for feedback.

Getting Started

It is not unusual for all parties to be a bit nervous when launching a project. Even though you have done a good job of selecting the consultants, you are probably worried about how successful they will be in your organization. Can they deliver what they have promised? Will you be able to give them the proper guidance and work effectively with them? They are probably worried about some of the same things.

Consultants are your guests, so help them feel comfortable. Begin with introductions, especially if not everyone knows each other. Introduce yourself first to set an example. Share your professional background, especially anything that will be particularly relevant to the project. If you feel comfortable, share something personal about yourself, perhaps an outside interest, where you grew up, something about your family. The goal is to try to connect with others. Let everyone introduce themselves in a similar way.

Clarify the meeting objectives and give an overview of the agenda. Make sure that everyone has the agenda as well as any other materials that will be necessary for the meeting. Check with others to see whether they want to add anything to the agenda.

The kick-off is a great time to compliment the consultants and their proposal and explain why you selected them. This public recognition can help reassure the consultants and begin to build the relationship.

Encourage an open dialogue. As you work through your agenda, take into account the balance of participation in the conversation. If this is a true partnership, you should not do all the talking. Neither should your consulting partners. What you hope for is a balance in the conversation, give-and-take. Make sure all participants have a voice.

Set the expectation early that you will want regular feedback that addresses both the project and the relationship. Encourage people to address concerns at any point. Explain that you will want to allow time at the end of the meeting to discuss what went well in the meeting and what should be improved for the future.

Before getting into the heart of the meeting, select a timekeeper. The timekeeper will help to ensure your meeting stays on track. Also select someone to take notes. It is often helpful to use a computer for note taking. When the meeting ends, there is no need to transcribe notes. You will be able to easily distribute the notes to everyone.

Clarifying the Objectives

Your consultants will probably want you to begin by clarifying the objectives of the project. Although you have had conversations about the objectives in the RFP and vendor selection process, it is important to repeat and clarify the objectives more fully at this point. The critical players on the project are now present, and you will want to launch the project with everyone having a common understanding of the goals. It is also not unusual for the team to get clearer and more specific about the objectives with more conversation.

As in every good training design, there needs to be alignment between the objectives of the training program and the objectives of the organization. How will this program increase sales or profitability? Will it improve productivity or customer service? Does it have the potential to reduce employee turnover? What are the important strategic objectives of your organization and how will this program contribute?

Clarity of objectives leads to project success. It is not unusual for training managers to be unclear about objectives at the beginning of a project. You may have a general idea of what you want to accomplish. But you may not have a great deal of specificity at this point. Through conversation in the kick-off meeting, your consultants will probably help you clarify your objectives more fully. On the other hand, a more thorough needs assessment in which you gather data to clarify the objectives may need to be completed as part of the project.

If your project is a technology-based solution, your program objectives are even more important. The complexity of development and costs associated with developing technology-based programs require you to have very clear objectives before the design and development work can begin. Going back and revising programs based on a change in objectives becomes much more expensive than in traditional instruction. A change in objectives can also have significant impact on the project timeline.

Many consultants indicate that training managers often do not have clear and measurable objectives in mind when they begin a project. Objectives are often too broad or may be written in a way that would not lead to desired behavior change and results.

Training Manager, Technology Company

"I remember when I first hired Al to help with some program evaluation. He gave me a hard time about our course objectives. Said they weren't specific enough. I think the objective was something like, 'increase market share by improving selling knowledge of our sales force.' Al said that the original objective might lead to a PowerPoint presentation about selling, not a skill-building course that could really improve the selling skills of our sales force. He helped us refine the objectives. We ended up with something more quantitative, like 'see a 10 percent increase in penetration in our existing customer base, which would lead to a 3 percent increase in market share.' The program was rigorous. It taught sales reps how to analyze their accounts for additional opportunity and how to present their ideas to existing clients. There was extensive casework and role-play practice."

Lesson: Objectives pave the way to project success. Consultants can help you clarify objectives, ensuring you get a better return on your training investment. Work closely with your consultants to ensure objectives are clearly articulated and understood by the entire team.

You do not need to have all the answers. This is one of the many reasons you are engaging a consultant. The process you go through with the consultant to clarify the objectives of a program will be important to the project. The conversation and the subsequent revisions to your original objectives provide you with an opportunity to learn and strengthen your capabilities to design future programs.

Evaluation Plan

Evaluating program effectiveness is the area that often gets the least attention. At best, it seems to be an afterthought. Many training managers try to figure out how they will measure a program after it is implemented. The best time to plan your evaluation is at the beginning of a project. For every project, there should be a discussion that begins with the questions, "When this project is complete, how will we know if we are successful? What will be the key success indicators?"

Although you may not take the time to determine all the details of your plan to evaluate the success of the project in your kick-off meeting, there should be some discussion of this topic. At a minimum, determine when you will build your evaluation plan. After all, the evaluation plan is based on the objectives you establish at the beginning of the project. Chapter 14 on evaluation provides more discussion of this topic.

Context Setting

Organization Development Consultant

"Our firm was invited to implement a 360-degree feedback process for a public utility. The project was supporting a cultural change focused on improving customer service. We spent significant time gathering input to build the competency model and plan the implementation. We felt we could build greater receptivity through a training initiative. I was surprised when we met with the first group that there was so much resistance. Evidently, these same employees had participated in an organization improvement project with consultants two years before. They had been interviewed and there was a breach of confidentiality. I wish the training manager had filled us in. We would have taken a totally different approach."

Lesson: Carefully consider the project in the context of the organization's history and share relevant issues with the consultants.

One of the most important roles you play is helping your consultants understand the context in which they are working. Without this information it is hard for consultants to be successful. Withholding important information regarding the context in which the consultants will be operating can lead to project failure. The worksheet in Exhibit 9.2, Context Setting, helps you consider some of the information that you should communicate to your consulting partners.

Exhibit 9.2. Context Setting.

Instructions: This worksheet can help you think through important information about your organization that should be communicated to your consulting partners as you launch your project. By discussing the context for the project, you are improving the likelihood that your consulting partners will help you develop solutions that meet the needs of your organization.

Project: _____

Factors	Notes
Industry	
• Competition	
• Trends	
• Industry issues	
• Other	
Organization	
• Mission	
• Strategic objectives	
• Priorities	
• Cultural issues	
• Leadership	

Exhibit 9.2. Context Setting *(continued)*

Factors	Notes
• Organization structure	
• Job descriptions	
• Jargon	
• Other	
Project	
• Importance of project	
• Relationship to other initiatives	
• Sponsors	
• Key players/their attitudes	
• Plan to build sponsorship	
• Political realities	
• Landmines	
• Obstacles	
• Past successes/failures	
• Other	

Sharing information of this nature may seem like telling too much. You may even feel uncomfortable discussing any dysfunction in your organization. But imagine what it would be like for you work without an in-depth understanding of your organization. You could not be successful. Remember, every organization has its strengths and weaknesses. Your openness helps the consultants relate better to the people in your organization. It helps them position the work more effectively as they meet with other employees during the various phases of the project. It will also enable them to recommend certain solutions over others if they understand the realities of your organization. Your consultants have worked in many organizations and will probably not be surprised by the issues you face.

If your initiative is a technology-based project, you will want to discuss the history of technology in your organization. Here are some questions you might consider:

- How supportive is the IT department?
- How comfortable are employees with technology?
- How much experience do they have?
- What kinds of experiences have employees had previously with technology?
- How open are employees to this initiative?
- Are there differences in capabilities between different employee groups, and how will this impact the project?
- How widely dispersed are computers?
- What kind of hardware is available?
- Will certain software be required?
- Is there consistency of hardware throughout your organization?
- What network capabilities do you have?

All of these issues will impact your solution. Helping your consultants understand the history is important to the ultimate success of your initiative.

Setting context is not just necessary at the beginning of a project. You operate in a dynamic organization. There are constant changes that may impact your initiative. Perhaps there are changes in leadership or organization structure. Priorities may shift. It is important to keep your consulting partners informed about changes that may impact the project. Context setting is an ongoing responsibility of the training manager when working with consultants.

Training Manager, Pharmaceutical Firm

"I hired a consultant to facilitate a program that had been running for over a year. I spent a day with the consultant briefing him on the program and the organization. We reviewed the course materials and discussed the participants who would be attending. I filled him in on some recent changes, the culture, job descriptions, and related initiatives. I had the consultant observe the class before teaching it. I also arranged for him to interview various managers in the company who would be attending. After conducting his first session, the consultant called to thank me for doing such a thorough job of orienting him. He got very positive feedback from participants on his ability to make the program relevant."

Lesson: After engaging consultants, be sure to thoroughly orient them to your organization.

Project Sponsorship

If you have strong project sponsorship, you are more likely to achieve project success. As part of context setting, you should describe the project sponsors and level of support you have for the program. Because sponsorship is critically important, allow time to discuss how you will build support for the initiative prior to implementation. Determine who needs to provide support and their current level of commitment. There is a big difference between the executive who says the training is important and the executive who will attend the program first to demonstrate its importance to the organization.

As consultants are working in the organization in the assessment and development phases, they can help build sponsorship by helping others understand the importance of the initiative. They can help management understand how to become involved to ensure success. In order for consultants to help sell programs internally, they need to understand who to influence and how best to influence them. Make a discussion of sponsorship an item on your agenda in the kick-off meeting.

Outlining the Project Plan

After clarifying the objectives, determining project success factors, and discussing the context, you can then focus on a plan for the project. You and your consultants should discuss the various phases of the project and the timing associated with it. Of course, how the project should proceed is highly variable depending on the type of project. You will have ideas on how to proceed. Your consultants will also make recommendations. You may find the following phases of a project useful as you plan your initiative with your consultants:

- *Assessment of Need.* Clarifying the request and analyzing the problem, often through interviews, surveys, observations, or analysis of relevant data

- *Design.* Setting the objectives, planning how to evaluate the effectiveness of the project, and determining the approach to solve the problem

- *Development.* Developing the intervention or writing the program; often includes a pilot of the program

- *Implementation.* Launching and executing the program or process

- *Evaluation.* Conducting the evaluation to measure the project's success and its impact on the organization

Collaboration and project planning go hand in hand. You bring certain expertise. You know the people in your organization, the culture, what will work, and what will not work. Your consultants bring certain expertise. They have the benefit of having worked in many organizations and many industries. They have a wide range of experiences to share.

There will be many decisions to make for each of the phases of your project. You will probably not have time to make all of these decisions in the kick-off meeting. But some discussion of each of these phases will help bring greater clarity to the team regarding how the project should proceed, the kinds of decisions that will need to be made, and the timing associated with each phase. By having this initial discussion, you will jointly shape the direction of the project.

Timing

Timing is another consideration. You will have certain deadlines that you will need to meet. Is there a certain date by which the project must be complete because of commitments you have made to your management or the cycle of the business year? You also may be working on other projects that will require your attention. Your consultants are probably working on a variety of projects for other organizations. It is important to discuss the amount of time it will take to do each phase of the project. You may not know exactly what it will take at this point, but it is a good idea to begin to plan together.

Make each other aware of your other projects and constraints that may affect the timing of the project. Are vacations scheduled? Are there certain times you or they will or will not be available? At what point will it be important to meet again? Should these meetings be held in person or can they be handled by phone? Where will the meetings take place? If at all possible, get future meetings on the calendar. Scheduling these meetings at the kick-off ensures everyone's availability.

Timing is even more important to consider in planning technology-based projects. These projects seem to take more time in terms of design, development, review, feedback, piloting, and revisions because of the precision and detail orientation that is required to produce a quality product. Therefore, be realistic in planning the timing for the project. You will want to allow sufficient time to be sure you can produce an excellent product that will be well accepted in your organization. Of course, you do not always control the timing. The time required for development must also be balanced with the needs of the organization. For example, your organization may plan to launch a new system that will have a technology-based training program to support it. The training will need to be ready concurrent with the system launch.

By the end of the kick-off meeting, you will have a general sense of the phases of the project and the associated timing. The next step is to build a comprehensive time and action calendar so that everyone involved in the project fully understands project expectations.

Roles and Responsibilities

In the kick-off meeting, jointly clarify roles and responsibilities. You bring certain knowledge, skills, and preferences to the project, and so do your consultants. You will want to look at all the aspects of the project and determine which team members are best suited to the various tasks.

Some of the issues to be resolved regarding roles and responsibilities may include:

- Who will serve as project manager?
- Who will develop the time and action calendar?
- Given the time and action calendar and other workload issues, who is available to do the various tasks?
- If interviews are needed, who will prepare the interview guides, who will schedule the appointments, and who will conduct the interviews?
- Who will conduct any needed research or benchmarking?
- Who will analyze the data and prepare reports that are needed?
- Who will design the program?
- Who will review the project design at select stages with key stakeholders?
- Who will develop materials?
- If the program is technology-based, who will build the plan for testing, and who will need to be involved in testing?
- Who will oversee the pilot?

- Who will deliver the training?
- Who will handle administrative work such as word processing and duplicating materials?
- Who will build the plan to evaluate the program?
- Who will conduct the evaluation?

There should be clarity in assigning roles and responsibilities. There should also be flexibility. Budget and available resources may dictate whether the training manager, members of the training department, or consultants take on a particular task. In assigning responsibilities, consider who is the most capable. Also consider who might learn from the experience.

It is important to have a single point of contact from each of the organizations to serve as project manager. Having one person from each organization taking the lead minimizes communication breakdowns. This arrangement does not mean that all communications need to flow through the two project managers. As roles are assigned, the appropriate people from either organization can communicate directly with each other as needed. If problems surface and cannot be resolved among the team members, the project managers from the consulting firm and the training department can work things out.

You will find that some tasks can be handled by multiple members of the team. For example, it might be a good idea to have several members of the team conduct the interviews for a needs assessment. If you have people from both your organization and the consulting firm conduct these interviews, you may be able to interview more people than the budget would seem to allow. It would also give more team members first-hand knowledge of the problem and, therefore, yield better results when the team generates potential solutions.

Be clear about who will handle administrative work such as scheduling interviews and meetings, ordering supplies, duplicating materials, registration, and mailings. Either the training department or the consultants may take on the administrative work, depending on the available resources and what has been negotiated in the contract.

As you delegate responsibility on the project to individuals in your organization, be sure they have the expertise and clout to get the job done.

Consultants describe frustration and wasted time when projects are delegated to internals who do not have the knowledge or framework to adequately support the consultant's work.

Plans for Communications

Effective project teams maintain a steady flow of communication. Successful partnerships are highly dependent on the frequency of communication. Take time on your agenda to determine a communications plan. The frequency of contact will depend on the complexity of the project and your timeline. It is not uncommon to have a weekly telephone update for a complex project. The call is an opportunity to communicate progress, discuss problems that may have surfaced, and plan for the future. Have a discussion about the frequency of contact and schedule the phone calls or meetings your team feels are necessary. It is easier to schedule time at this point, rather than closer to the meetings when team members' calendars may already be full.

When discussing communications, acknowledge the likelihood of conflict arising. Invite team members to surface concerns they have at any point in the project. There is no need to wait until a regularly scheduled meeting to discuss a problem. Stress the fact that conflict needs to be resolved so that it does not interfere with the outcomes of the project. The chapter on managing conflict (Chapter 16) provides a more in-depth look at the causes of conflict and ways to deal effectively with it.

Next Steps

Your meeting has probably been quite productive. It is important to allow time at the end of the meeting to discuss next steps. You do not want to lose momentum on the project. Typical next steps that follow a kick-off meeting include:

- Sending the notes of the kick-off meeting to all participants
- Updating management on the progress of the project
- Drafting the time and action calendar
- Sending related materials for review to the meeting participants
- Planning for the next meeting or scheduling follow-up phone calls

Partnership Update

The partnership update provides a structure for you to communicate openly, build trust, and ensure alignment between you and your consulting partners. The more open your communications, the more likely you are to build trust and collaborate. The partnership update is a time set aside for the project team to stop action, review what has happened, and to learn from the experience. You may be familiar with a similar approach, the after action review, which is used in the military.

Build the partnership update into your project plan. At a minimum, plan to conduct the partnership update at the end of each significant phase of the project. These scheduled updates should not prevent you from sharing feedback with your consulting partners at any point throughout the project. In all likelihood, the end of the kick-off meeting is the first time on the project you will provide each other with feedback through the partnership update. Future partnership updates should be scheduled at a time when all team members are available.

The communication at the partnership update should be on two levels— the project and the relationship. Be sure to allow sufficient time for this discussion. Keep the feedback balanced, highlighting the positives as well as areas for improvement.

You and your team members should determine how you will conduct the partnership update. Some organizations prefer a formal process. Others handle the update in a more informal way. Sometimes the formality depends on the size of the project. If you are outsourcing your entire training function, your approach will probably be formal and set at regular intervals. If you are outsourcing a smaller project, you may opt for a less formal process. The worksheet in Exhibit 9.3, Partnership Update: Kick-Off Meeting, may be a helpful tool to plan your first partnership update.

Exhibit 9.3. Partnership Update: Kick-Off Meeting.

Instructions: This worksheet can help you plan the partnership update that follows your project kick-off meeting. It can be used in association with the Service Partnership Scorecard (Exhibit 9.4). Use the notes column on the right for ideas you would like to discuss with your consulting partners. Document suggestions for improvement or agreements at the bottom of the page and bring these notes to future partnership updates.

Project: _____

Agenda	Notes
Explain purpose of partnership update	• Strengthen the partnership • Get feedback on the project • Get feedback on the effectiveness of the team
Introduce Service Partnership Scorecard (if you plan to use it)	• Structured way to evaluate the partnership and provide each other with feedback • Jointly identify the criteria for the scorecard
Discuss criteria that will be important to a successful partnership (if taking a more informal approach and not using partnership scorecard)	• Regular communications • Confront conflict openly • Timeliness

Discuss effectiveness of kick-off meeting
  • What worked?
  • What did not work and why	

Provide feedback to each other using partnership scorecard or established criteria for partnership success (listed above)	

Future focus
  • What concerns does anyone have about the project or the team?
  • What does the team need to do to ensure the success of the project?	

Agreements:	

Formal Partnership Update. At the first update, explain the purpose of the meeting to everyone involved. Let members of the team know that the goal is to get feedback on the project and on the effectiveness of the team. The discussion is designed to keep the project on track, build partnerships, and get the best possible results.

You will probably want to use a structured methodology for soliciting feedback. The partnership scorecard may be helpful. The partnership scorecard is a rating sheet whereby the training manager and consultants can list the criteria on which they would like to evaluate each other. (See Exhibit 9.4 for a sample that has been provided by Development Dimensions International.) Criteria should be negotiated between the training manager and consultants at the kick-off meeting. They should select criteria that are important to project success and ensure strong partnerships. Each project will have its own set of criteria.

Exhibit 9.4. Sample Service Partnership Scorecard.

DDI®

Name of Client: _____ Date: _____

Client Feedback to Consultant						Consultant Feedback to Client				
1	2	3	x4	5	**Professional/Technical Expertise**	1	2	3	4	x5

Demonstrates technical and professional skills and knowledge in project and implementation.

Your IT support team handled themselves professionally in every interaction with our technical group. We received feedback that your team was very knowledgeable. This made the implementation go more smoothly than we had anticipated.	We are very impressed with your team. They have a strong understanding of the business and how to implement change effectively. It helps to work with an experienced group.

1	2	3	4	x5	**Consultative Approach/Analysis**	1	2	3	4x	5

Seeks input on objectives, needs, issues, and constraints, then identifies and discusses alternatives to reach mutual agreement on the best approach.

We take a consultative approach. Your questions helped us better understand the issues and challenged our thinking. I appreciated the way you involved us in the process. It also helped to explore various approaches to the implementation plan.	You and your team are open to new ideas and fresh approaches. You seem to always seek input on how to make initiatives more successful and take a collaborative approach to problem solving.

1 = Unsatisfactory 2 = Concerned 3 = Meets Expectations 4 = Exceeds Expectations 5 = Delighted

Exhibit 9.4. Sample Service Partnership Scorecard *(continued)*

1	2	3	4	x5	Service Orientation	1	2	3	4	x5
					**Demonstrated "can do" attitude and willingness to go above and beyond to meet and/or exceed expectations.**					

I think the project went as well as it did because of the "can do" attitude of your team. As we were planning the project, they shared their experiences from the past. This helped us understand the issues we faced. Whatever we requested, they provided. They worked long and hard to make sure we were ready before the launch. Thank you very much.	Your team is focused on delivering the best possible program to your organization. They have high energy and attention to detail. They are always looking for ways to satisfy the customer. We learned from them in the process!

1	2	x3	4	5	Project Management	1	2	3	x4	5
					Uses a process for planning and managing work and resources to reach a desired end result on time, within budget, and according to specifications. Monitors progress and makes necessary adjustments or improvements to ensure project success. Communicates project variances from project specifications to ensure completion within existing constraints or gain mutual agreement on changes to the scope of work.					

You put together a very comprehensive project plan. I think we all understood our roles. I appreciated our project updates. An area for improvement would be to meet more frequently. We probably could have discovered the challenge in the budget more quickly and resolved it sooner.	You and your team always met your commitments to us. You were always aware of issues in the organization that might get us off track. You raised these on our project calls and this helped to improve our final results.

1 = Unsatisfactory 2 = Concerned 3 = Meets Expectations 4 = Exceeds Expectations 5 = Delighted

Exhibit 9.4. Sample Service Partnership Scorecard *(continued)*

DDI⬤

1	2	3	x4	x5	Communication	1	2	3	4	x5

Listens, checks for understanding, and exchanges relevant and reliable information in a clear and appropriate manner. Communicates effectively and frequently to ensure appropriate level of involvement. Clearly explains technical information and implications.

Your team members are great communicators. They listen carefully and do not make assumptions. In our early meetings, they asked many questions to try to understand our culture and what would be most successful in our environment.	Your team has strong communication skills. People listen to each other and speak openly and honestly. When there are disagreements, you and your team raise the issues and treat others with respect.

1	2	3	4	x5	Responsiveness	1	2	3	x4	5

Responds in a timely and effective manner to requests for information, assistance or support

I was very pleased with your responsiveness. When I requested the project report sooner than you expected, your team was able to respond quickly. I know this was not easy to do and I appreciate the support.	During the research phase, your staff responded quickly to our requests for organization charts and reports. This helped us to be more knowledgeable as we met with others in your organization. We also found your administrative assistant particularly helpful. She helped with travel arrangements and followed up on materials that we shipped.

1 = Unsatisfactory 2 = Concerned 3 = Meets Expectations 4 = Exceeds Expectations 5 = Delighted

Exhibit 9.4. Sample Service Partnership Scorecard *(continued)*

1	2	3	x4	x5	Partnership	1	2	3	x4	x5

Partnerships are established by dealing with each other fairly, openly, and honestly. DDI has developed key principles to support developing effective partnerships. These principles include:

- Involve the customer
- Share thoughts, feelings, and rationale
- Listen and respond with empathy

- Maintain or enhance self-esteem
- Ask for help and encourage involvement
- Provide support without removing responsibility

To what extent has the DDI team modeled these core values and developed an effective partnership?

You are excellent partners. When you tell us you will do something, you always follow through. We have great trust in you. You were also very honest with us about some of the problems you thought we would face. This honesty helped us prepare and overcome the obstacles.	We are very pleased with our partnership with you. You challenged us to deliver a high-quality product, and were always there to support us with what we needed to make this happen. When the budget became an issue, you communicated in a respectful way and helped us find ways to solve the problem. We felt that you were open to our help and that we could count on your team for help as well.

1	2	3	x4	5	Understand Client's Needs	1	2	3	4	x5

Understands client's processes, priorities, and objectives and supports client's objectives. Client provides information about the organization, people, needs, etc. Consultant provides quality solutions that address client's needs.

Your process for interviewing the key stakeholders in our company helped you to understand our priorities and our objectives. This helped us position the program successfully. I think the participants understand why the skills we are teaching are so important to the future of the company.	In the kick-off meeting, you did an excellent job of explaining your organization, the culture, your leadership, the target audience, and the political issues we would face. This positioned us to get the most out of our interviews. All requests from you and your team were fulfilled in a timely manner.

1 = Unsatisfactory 2 = Concerned 3 = Meets Expectations 4 = Exceeds Expectations 5 = Delighted

Name   Date   Name   Date

Once you have established the criteria for the scorecard, take time to rate each other based on your interactions in the kick-off meeting. Before providing feedback using the scorecard, have a general discussion giving each other some overall impressions of what it has been like to work together at the kick-off meeting. What has worked well and what could be improved? Then provide feedback to each other going item by item on the partnership scorecard. Explain your rating for the first item and give specific examples. Ask your consulting partners to give their rating for the same item. Then have an open discussion for clarification. In the discussion be sure to actively listen to your partners' feedback. This is not a time for defensiveness. It is an opportunity to learn how to make the partnership more effective. Be sure to highlight positives as well as negatives such as, "I feel like I learn something new every time we interact. You have broadened my perspective. At the same time I am worried about our ability to meet our deadlines. I had hoped we would be further along at this point."

Once you have discussed all the ratings on the partnership scorecard, summarize your understandings. Jointly make commitments to each other on ways you plan to work together in the future. Document these commitments for future conversations. This partnership scorecard can serve as the springboard for partnership updates in the future.

Informal Partnership Update. You may feel it is more appropriate to use an informal approach for a partnership update. You can have an informal discussion instead. What is important is to be sure conversations about the project and the partnership take place with all team members.

Get the discussion started in the same way you would if you were conducting a more formal meeting. Make sure everyone knows the purpose of the discussion and that you would like to have similar discussions throughout the project. You will probably not use a tool such as the partnership scorecard. However, it is still a good idea to jointly discuss criteria for working together effectively. You can refer back to these criteria at future partnership updates. Lead a discussion and consider using some of the following questions:

- How did the kick-off meeting go?
- What worked? What did not work? Why?
- What can we do in the future to work more effectively together?
- What concerns, if any, do you have about the project or our team that you may not have mentioned?
- What do you think will be most important to ensure the success of our partnership?

Encourage all members of the team to participate. Compliment the team when things are mentioned that are going well. Be sure the team gives specific examples so everyone on the team understands what is working and why. Do not hesitate to encourage the team to address issues that are getting in the way of working together successfully. Be sure they are specific about areas in which the team needs to improve.

In a high functioning team, you will want the business of the team conducted in the presence of the full team. However, there may be times in either a formal or informal partnership update at which you determine that it is best not to confront something in front of the entire team. Perhaps there is a sensitive issue with one of the members of the team that is best dealt with privately with that individual. This takes judgment, with the primary goal being to maintain the partnership and positive working relationships.

Take notes on the points that are discussed. As with a more formal approach, plan to bring these notes to future partnership update meetings and check on the progress that is made. Having these notes available will make it easier for you to help keep the team on track and work toward improving the partnership over time. Questions you will want to consider at future meetings might include:

- What progress have we made on the issues we discussed previously?
- How is the team functioning now as compared to previous meetings?

Training Director, Financial Services Firm

"At a kick-off meeting of a new project, one of the consultants kept taking cell phone calls throughout the day. He apologized each time. I didn't say anything, because we were just getting to know each other. Over the life of the project, the interruptions continued. I ended up feeling angry. At the pilot, the consultant used every break to check messages. I was really upset, because I felt he should have been available to participants during the breaks. By the time I confronted the issue, I was way too angry. Maybe it was the stress of the pilot. I probably did more to damage the relationship by waiting than I would have if I had confronted it right up-front."

Lesson: Address conflict quickly. The partnership update provides a way to confront difficult issues. Do not wait for the partnership update if an issue surfaces.

In this chapter you have explored how to launch a project successfully. Through the kick-off meeting, you began to examine some of the issues of project management. Chapter 10 provides a more in-depth discussion of this topic.

■ ■ ■ ■

Key Ideas

- A kick-off meeting will help you launch your project effectively and build partnerships with your consultants.

- Work with your consulting partners to plan the location and agenda for your kick-off meeting.

- Establish partnerships with all members of the project team, even those who work behind the scenes in the consulting firm.

- Arrange to have your consulting partners sign confidentiality agreements before beginning the work.

- Pay close attention to logistical arrangements (travel, security passes, room set-up, and equipment) for the kick-off meeting so you can focus attention on the most important aspects of the project. Attention to detail in logistics also signals to your partners the importance of good customer service.

- Include the appropriate people in your meeting. If your project is technology-based, it is especially important to include representatives of IT.

- Begin your meeting with introductions, working to help people feel comfortable and build the team. Encourage an open dialogue.

- Clarify the objectives of the project.

- Determine measures of success and a preliminary evaluation plan.

- Help the consultants understand your organization by spending significant time setting the context for the project.

- If your project is technology-based, help consultants understand the history of technology in your organization.

- Discuss sponsorship for your project. Identify the key sponsors and their current level of support.

- Discuss a preliminary project plan, including timing, roles and responsibilities, communication, and next steps.

- Conduct a partnership update to end the kick-off meeting.

Project Management

Importance of Project Management

Experienced training managers point to effective project management as an ingredient of successful partnerships. Elements of project management that are important to partnerships include clarifying expectations, careful monitoring of progress, anticipating obstacles, and a willingness to confront difficult situations. Whether projects are large or small, simple or complex, skillful project management can make the difference between an initiative that achieves its objectives and one that does not.

Project management is especially important to technology-based projects, where the risks are greater than on traditional training projects. These projects often have more resources that require coordination. There are instructional designers, graphic artists, subject-matter experts, programmers, and other project team members. Reviews and approvals on content are more detailed and extensive. Budgets are frequently larger, and revisions can be more time-consuming and expensive. When technology-based projects get off track, budgets can be exhausted quickly, and there may be insufficient time to make revisions to meet project deadlines.

To avoid major cost overruns and to achieve project objectives, be certain that every project is managed carefully. This section focuses on the role project management plays in strong partnerships. The following aspects of project management are discussed:

- Role of the project manager
- Managing scope
- Managing risk
- Managing resources
- Managing communications

Some of these topics were also covered in Chapter 9, Launching the Project, since they are issues that training managers and consultants discuss in the early stages of a project. All issues of project management cannot be resolved in that first meeting. They are generally explored at the kick-off meeting and finalized in subsequent meetings.

Vice President, Training, Hospitality Industry

"I'm not particularly detailed-oriented, so the contract I negotiated with our consultants included project management. We were implementing a program for high-potentials. The project manager from the consulting firm coordinated resources in her organization. I decided to share project management responsibility in my organization with one of my direct reports. I handled the strategic aspects of the project, things like setting goals, determining content, and confronting conflicts that surfaced. My direct report handled the tactical elements, monitoring the time and action calendar, reviewing the contract with our in-house attorney, and ensuring that the bills got paid on time. The approach worked well since it was based on our strengths. We had a good partnership."

Lesson: A shared model of project management can ensure a smooth-running project and a strong partnership.

Role of the Project Manager

In the early stages of a project, determine who will play the role of project manager based on the capabilities of those involved. In determining who takes responsibility for project management, consider that project managers need to be well-organized and detail-oriented. They need to be able to develop and monitor time and action calendars and budgets. They should be individuals who value collaboration and regular communication and who willingly confront difficult situations. You may choose to play this role, a member of your team may do so, or you may request these services from your consulting partner. It is often the case that project management is a shared responsibility. There is a project manager who represents your organization, and there is a project manager who represents the consulting firm. Having a single point of contact from both organizations helps eliminate redundancy, streamline communication, and avoid confusion.

If possible, identify who will take responsibility for project management in advance of finalizing your contract, because there are cost implications associated with this decision. A complex project takes many hours of project management. It is typical for consulting firms to charge for these services on complex projects, so you may see a line item in the consultant's budget for project management.

On technology-based projects, it is a best practice to be sure that the project manager in the consulting firm is not the programmer. That project manager can serve as a buffer and be the go-to person if you are dissatisfied, can keep track of internal resources, and can help you understand technology constraints.

Managing Scope

Consultant, Evaluation Expert

"A training manager hired me to evaluate a program. We outlined the scope and determined that the project would include pre-training surveys, post-training surveys, and follow-up interviews. The survey data needed to be analyzed and a final report written and communicated to management. We agreed that I would serve as lead project manager, draft the surveys, and analyze the data. The training manager's team would explain the expectations for the evaluation to participants and their management, conduct the surveys and interviews, write the final report, and communicate results to management.

"In the middle of the project, the training manager approached me and asked for advice on evaluating another program. I gave the training manager some advice. A few weeks later the training manger asked me to review a questionnaire for the second program. I reviewed it and gave some feedback. The next time she asked for advice, I felt I had to let the training manager know that her request was beyond the original scope of our contract. I offered to help on the second project, but explained that we would have to renegotiate the contract and the fee. Knowing she needed the support, the training manager agreed and modified the contract to include the extra project."

Lesson: Be aware when you step beyond the scope of a project. Respect the consultant and do not take advantage of the partnership. Be willing to modify your contract to reflect the additional work.

The scope of the project is usually outlined in the RFP. It is furthered clarified in the contract and then in the early stages of the project. As you and your consultants define project scope, you are identifying project objectives, deliverables, what the consulting firm will do, and what the internal training department will do. When defining the project scope, you can also identify what will not be included in the project. Defining scope helps determine the cost of the project.

Project managers help to control projects by managing scope over the life of the projects. They make sure that the activities that are completed are within the scope, or defined boundaries, of the project. They try to help the team avoid scope creep, when the project gets larger and members of the team begin to do more than what has been outlined in the original project definition. The term scope creep is used, because it is not uncommon for it to go unnoticed by the team that the project is expanding beyond its original bounds. If the project exceeds the original scope, it must be addressed clearly as soon as it is discerned. The project manager generally calls attention to the situation, although any member of the team can do so. Then it is up to the team to determine whether they will, in fact, expand the project. If so, they will need to renegotiate the scope and modify the plan to reflect changes in deliverables, time, and cost.

Managing Risk

Part of project management is managing risk. What could go wrong, and how could it be prevented? It is important to do contingency planning in the early stages of a project. The numbers and kinds of problems that could surface are too numerous to mention.

Explore the risks with your consulting partners. The Risk Assessment Worksheet (Exhibit 10.1) may be helpful. Together you can consider potential obstacles and plan ways to overcome them before they derail your initiative. Because of their external perspective, your consulting partners may be able to anticipate problems more easily than you can.

Managing Resources

Project management is largely about managing resources, including time, people, and the budget. Project managers begin by building a plan, including delegating responsibility, determining time frames, and allocating budgets. Then they monitor progress of the project, ensuring quality and timeliness within budget constraints. They also remove obstacles and help to confront and resolve issues that surface.

Building the Project Plan

Once the scope of the project is determined and the risks have been assessed, the project manager usually builds a project plan. Project plans are particularly important on complex initiatives. Exhibit 10.2 is a sample project plan. It includes selected tasks from a complex leadership development program. Using an Excel spreadsheet enables you to list tasks by category or date.

The plan typically includes the following:

- Comprehensive listing of all the activities that need to be completed in order to achieve the overall objectives of the project

- Assignments of who will complete each of the tasks

- Timing of when each task needs to be completed to meet the overall project deadline

- Place to record task completion

- Place to indicate notes or identify issues

Exhibit 10.1. Risk Assessment Worksheet.

Instructions: This worksheet can help you and your consulting partners explore risks to your project. Through thorough risk assessment, you will be able to do contingency planning and overcome obstacles that could interfere with project success. Consider the questions below and determine ways to address challenges on your project.

Project: _____

Potential Risks	Anticipated Obstacles	Ways to Address
Are changes in the organization expected that could impact the project?		
Could other initiatives impact the perception or timing of the project?		
Are budget cuts expected that could impact the project?		
Are there individuals who do not support the project? How could you get their support?		
If this is a technology-based project, do you have the support of the IT department?		
Is there sufficient talent on the team? Are additional resources needed?		
Are members of the team vulnerable in any way? Do you anticipate turnover?		
Are there competing projects, workload, or travel that could impact performance?		

Exhibit 10.2. Sample Project Plan.
2005 Leadership Development Program*

	Category	Description	Responsibility	Date Start	Date Due	Status	Notes
1	Assess	Send assessment packet to participants	Gus	4/29	4/29	complete	
2	Assess	Contact HR and schedule interviews	Coaches	4/29	5/6	complete	Call Jim after 5/2
3	Assess	Participants nominate raters for 360	Participants	5/2	5/9	complete	
4	Assess	Complete autobiography	Participants	5/2	5/16	complete	
5	Assess	Write assessment reports	Coaches	6/27	7/13	not started	
6	Coach	Match coaches and participants	Donna	4/25	4/25	complete	
7	Coach	Call with coaches to review process	Donna/Coaches	5/2	5/6	complete	
8	Coach	Coaches call participants to introduce themselves	Coaches	5/2	5/9	complete	
9	Coach	Coaching session 1—assessment	Coaches	6/13	7/8	in progress	
10	Coach	Conduct follow-up calls with HR re: assessment	Coaches	7/25	8/5	not started	
11	Deliver	Send session pre-course	Melissa	7/15	7/15	not started	
12	Deliver	Session walkthrough	Donna/Melissa/ Susan/Daniel	7/20	7/20	not started	In NYC
13	Deliver	Facilitate session	Daniel/Michael	8/14	8/19	not started	
14	Deliver	Follow-up videoconference	Donna/Daniel	10/3	11/18	not started	

*This sample includes selected tasks from a project plan.

Exhibit 10.2. Sample Project Plan *(continued)*

	Category	Description	Responsibility	Date Start	Date Due	Status	Notes
15	Develop	Determine design revisions	Donna/Melissa	3/4	3/4	complete	
16	Develop	Schedule external speakers	Melissa	4/1	5/6	in progress	
17	Develop	Design review	Team	5/16	5/17	complete	In Detroit, start at 8:30
18	Develop	Collect speaker biographies	Melissa	5/19	5/27	in progress	
19	Develop	Revise program materials	Daniel/Betty	5/19	5/31	in progress	Discuss graphics and slide template
20	Mgmt	Order binders	Kathy	4/11	4/11	complete	
21	Mgmt	Plan evening dinners/social activities	Melissa	4/11	5/6	complete	
22	Mgmt	Set up program information on website	Melissa	4/25	4/28	complete	
23	Mgmt	Plan daily menus	Melissa	5/2	5/31	not started	
24	Mgmt	Finalize travel and hotel for participants	Melissa	7/11	7/15	not started	
25	Orient	Draft orientation material	Donna/Betty	4/12	4/18	complete	
26	Orient	Hold boss/HR orientation conference call	Donna	4/26	4/26	complete	1:00 p.m. eastern
27	Orient	Hold participant orientation conference call	Donna	4/28	4/28	complete	

Make sure the project plan is easily accessible to all members of the team. You may want to use a software package such as Microsoft Project, which is designed for project management. Project management software can help you set up your project plans and manage your resources, particularly on complex projects. You might also consider building your project plan using an online spreadsheet.

In the spirit of partnership, the project plan is often developed jointly by the training manager, or whoever is acting as project manager, and the consultant. One of them will list all activities they can think of that need to be completed. The other will review and modify the list as needed. They will also identify when each task needs to be completed and who should take primary responsibility for completion of a particular task. Collaborating on the plan builds the partnership and helps the team avoid gaps. It is best for the entire team to finalize the plan to ensure that nothing is missing and that time frames are realistic.

When you assign team members to tasks, be sure to consider expertise, interest, and availability. There is a more detailed discussion of project roles and responsibilities in Chapter 9, Launching the Project.

Technology-Based Project Plans. On complex technology-based projects such as web or computer-based training design, there may be two project plans if a consulting firm is doing the development. The consulting firm may have an internal project plan that includes computer programming, graphic design, internal reviews, and testing. The second project plan might be the one that is used between the training manager and the consulting firm. It might be more global and address key milestones that are important to both organizations.

Whether there is one plan or two, it is important for the training manager to understand what it takes for the consulting firm to produce the course. Technology-based projects are more complex to develop than traditional classroom-based instruction. The level of complexity impacts the development time. When developing project plans for technology-based programs, work closely with your consultants to build realistic schedules for reviews and approval.

Especially if you are new to developing computer-based training or if you are working with a new firm, you will want to understand the course development process that your consulting firm uses. Ask to see samples of the kinds of materials you will need to review. Reviews will probably include the following:

- A high-level design

- A content outline

- A prototype

- Storyboards or actual screens and associated scripts

- The final program

You will want several people from your organization to participate in the review. These may include subject-matter experts, employees who represent the target population, their management, and other experts in training and development. Make sure they are aware of the schedule and know how much time it will take to do the review. Once their feedback is submitted, you or a member of your team will need to summarize the feedback and submit what is appropriate to the consulting firm. The consulting firm is relying on you and your team to give timely feedback so that they can make necessary changes and meet your project deadline.

Building the Project Budget

Depending on your organization and the particular project, you may or may not have the final project price negotiated until after the project plan is built. It is not uncommon to start a project without having the final budget set, because you are still determining scope, approach, project management responsibility, timing, and resources. There are also projects in which there is not a total project price negotiated, but a daily rate for consulting services.

By the time you have finalized the project plan, you and your consultants should be able to determine the price and build an associated budget. Pricing is usually based on the number of days of consulting time required, the level of expertise of the consultants, materials, the necessary travel, and any additional associated expenses. It is a best practice when planning the budget to tie the payment schedule to significant milestones or deliverables. Tying payments to deliverables helps to ensure accountability and keeps the project on track. The consultant must deliver a quality product to receive payment along the way.

Since you may not have a finalized project plan and budget until this point, you may not have actually signed a contract for services. If this is the case, your project plan and budget may actually end up as attachments to your contract.

Monitoring the Budget

Determine the frequency with which you need to check the budget based on your particular project. You will want to be sure that the project stays on track from a budget perspective, that consultant time is not exceeding the budget plan, and that bills are being processed in a timely fashion according to contract specifications. Since the project manager is frequently managing multiple projects, it can be helpful to use a simple bill payment tracking worksheet (Exhibit 10.3). After the contract is finalized, the project manager can simply transfer the payment schedule and associated deliverables to this worksheet. The project manager can make a notation on the worksheet every time a bill is paid. If a deliverable is unsatisfactory, this can be noted as well.

Be reasonable when managing the budget. Once you are in the design and development phase of a project, trust your consultants to manage the project within the stated budget. Feel free to ask how well the consultants are adhering to the budget. However, in the spirit of trusting and building partnerships, avoid micromanaging the budget. For example, you may have negotiated for a large-scale change initiative with a consulting firm. In putting together their proposal, they estimated the cost of various aspects of the project. It is not helpful to question them extensively on how well they are managing to keep within the budget for each component of the project. In reality, some segments may have cost more and some segments may have cost less. As long as they are keeping within the total contract price, this should be satisfactory.

Exhibit 10.3. Bill Payment Tracking Worksheet.

Instructions: Use this worksheet to track payments to vendors/consultants throughout the life of a project.

Project: _____

Consultant/Vendor: _____

Payment Due Date	Deliverable	Amount	Comments

Asking for a detailed accounting of every aspect of the project puts the emphasis on the less important aspects of the project. If a consultant has to justify every minute of time spent, then you will not get the best return on your investment. You want consultants to be free to do the creative work for which you have hired them. If you are constantly questioning the budget, you should ask yourself why. Are you feeling that the consultants are not meeting expectations? Are you dissatisfied with their performance? Is there something within you that causes you not to trust them? Are there other issues that should be addressed? If so, you should surface these issues in your regular communication so that they do not get in the way of success on the project.

Managing Communications

It is important to structure regular times for communication about the project. It is also important to establish the kind of atmosphere in which people will feel comfortable raising issues at any point that they feel is necessary.

Progress Checks

Some project managers believe that their only role is to ensure that each task on the project plan is completed according to the established timeline. Their focus is checking off the tasks as they are completed, but this is too simplistic an approach. Good project management requires regular progress checks and dialogue with the team to determine what is going well and where there may be issues that need to be addressed.

It is, therefore, not uncommon to schedule a weekly meeting either in person or by phone to check progress. The primary tool to guide the discussion can be your project plan. In addition, develop an agenda for each meeting by determining the priority issues. Here is a sample agenda for a regular check-in call or meeting:

- Informal check-in

  - Ask how team members are doing

  - Give an overview of the agenda

  - Ask for additional agenda items

- Review of project plan
  - Check to see whether project due dates have been met
  - Check on future tasks and associated due dates
- Address high-priority issues or problems that have surfaced
- Identify and discuss how to overcome any obstacles that are identified
- Ask team members to express concerns they may have or support they may need
- Plan topics for next meeting
- Celebrate progress

Work through your agenda at each check-in meeting. Address issues that surface. Plans rarely go as originally anticipated, particularly on large projects. Expect the unexpected. Be prepared to help your consultants when they need help. Ask for help if you need it. The stronger your partnerships, the easier it will be to resolve issues that are bound to surface.

Dealing with Conflict

A discussion of communications would not be complete without a discussion of managing conflict. Do not be surprised if conflict surfaces while working with consultants. Keeping the partnership foremost in your mind will help you resolve problems more easily. The goal should be win-win outcomes for you and your consultants. A good way to achieve solutions that work for both parties is to engage your partners in resolving difficult situations that arise. Refer to Chapter 16, Managing Conflict, for more detailed information on this subject.

Vice President, Organization Development and Training, Technology Company

"I hired a course developer to design a training program for the finance division of my company. The course developer was well-respected in the industry and had access to three subject-matter experts. The development took four months. I reviewed the program with our subject-matter experts and signed off on the training as each module was developed.

"Participants gave very negative feedback at the pilot. The course developer felt that he would need to invest an additional six weeks to correct the problems. He wanted to be paid for his time. I felt that the revisions were included in the original contract price. We had many discussions and eventually resolved our differences. We settled on a 50–50 split. Recognizing that I had reviewed and approved materials along the way, I agreed to pay the consultant for three weeks of additional work. We basically shared responsibility for the unsuccessful pilot."

Lesson: The spirit of partnership can help you when conflict surfaces. Be willing to compromise to achieve the results you need and maintain positive working relationships with your consulting partners.

Celebration

Do not wait for the end of the project to give positive feedback or celebrate. If your partners have met deadlines, solved problems creatively, or supported you in other ways, recognize them. Let them know what they have done that is helpful and how it is having a positive impact on the project. Projects are challenging, and it is motivating for people to know that they are appreciated for their contributions. Celebration is an important part of successful partnerships.

Director, Training, Government Agency

"I called David just to let him know how much I appreciate the work we are doing together. Whenever we run out of ideas, he always has another creative solution. The project is stressful, and I feel very supported. So I wanted to say thank you."

Lesson: Find opportunities along the way to give positive feedback. It will strengthen your partnership.

The Partnership Update

Your communications should include a regular partnership update. Refer to Chapter 9, Launching the Project, for a more detailed description of the partnership update. The partnership update is a structured approach to communications on the project team. It is usually conducted at the end of each phase of the project. It provides time for members of the team to stop action, review what has happened, make needed adjustments, and learn from the experience.

Project Management on Small Projects

You may manage small projects and deal with project management more informally. For example, you could engage a consultant to develop a half-day program on stress management. There is probably no need for a comprehensive project plan. Instead, you will negotiate due dates and reviews for the major components of the program. These might include:

- An outline
- Facilitator's guide
- Participant materials
- A walk-through

You would probably schedule a phone call or meeting at each review point to provide feedback.

In summary, the best projects probably have a balance of flexibility and control with a generous dose of trust. They are not necessarily the cheapest or most cost efficient, but they do seem to add the greatest value.

The first three chapters of Part 3 of this book, Positioning Consultants in Your Organization (Chapter 8), Launching the Project (Chapter 9), and Project Management (Chapter 10) have been designed to help you build a foundation and plan for the success of your project. Actual work on the project begins in Chapter 11, Assessment of Need.

Key Ideas

- Effective project management is an important ingredient of project success.

- Elements of project management that are important to partnerships include clarifying expectations, careful monitoring of project plans, anticipating obstacles, and a willingness to confront difficult situations.

- Successful project managers are well-organized and detail-oriented. They need to be able to develop and monitor time and action calendars and budgets. They should understand and value regular communications and be willing to deal with conflict.

- A shared model of project management between the consultant and the contracting organization can ensure a smooth-running project and strong partnership.

- Regular and meaningful communication between the training manager and the consultants will help the team achieve its objectives.

- Celebration strengthens the partnership.

11

Assessment of Need

Training Manager, Aerospace Industry

"Jim called asking me to put his front-line managers through an advanced program on confronting performance problems. He was frustrated that they weren't addressing issues. I like Jim and felt pressure to respond. But I was wondering what the problem was. His supervisors had already attended our course on coaching and addressing performance problems. The course was strong and gave lots of practice. Instead of scheduling his team for more training, I made an appointment to talk to Jim to find out more."

Lesson: Avoid the training quick fix by exploring the underlying causes of poor performance. Either independently or with the support of a consulting partner, conduct a needs assessment so that you can design a solution that gets results.

Leading training departments today are moving away from a training model to a performance consulting model. The best training managers understand that an accurate assessment of a problem is required to achieve a long-term, fundamental solution. They also realize that they no longer have the luxury to respond to every request with a training solution. Resources are limited. Training is not always the answer, but often just the quick fix. The training department loses credibility when training is applied and does not solve the problem. Skilled trainers understand that other factors can be at play when employees do not perform to expectations. Some of the questions you and your consulting partners will want to ask in a needs assessment to get to the root cause of performance problems include:

- Are the people well matched to the jobs?
- Are expectations clear?
- Do employees have the tools and equipment to do the jobs?
- Have training and feedback been provided?
- Does the reward system support the behavior you are seeking?
- What other factors in the system might be interfering with performance?

Many consultants indicate that their work with training managers is most successful when the training managers clearly understand the purpose of the work, how it relates to the organization's strategy, and associated underlying organizational issues. They are clear about the outcomes of the initiative and how success will be measured. This information is surfaced during the assessment phase. Without this data, it is difficult to develop a program that will have significant and lasting impact on the organization.

This chapter will explore the assessment phase of a project. It will help you determine whether or not to engage consultants for assessment, and if you do, how best to involve them. It will also help you deal with three critical assessment issues: access, buy-in, and methodology.

Should You Outsource Needs Assessment?

Consultants can add value to the needs assessment phase of a project. However, you or members of your team may choose to do this work instead. It is also possible, in the spirit of true partnership, to do the work jointly. The Strategic Sourcing Decision Model (Figure 3.1) and Exhibit 3.1, Making Sourcing Decisions, introduced in Chapter 3, can help you make the decision whether to outsource or in-source. As you consider the four knockout factors from the model—expertise, timing, cost, and context—and their associated tradeoffs, take the following into account:

Expertise

Do you have the expertise to design the assessment process, or is this a time when you would benefit from engaging a consultant? Depending on your experience, you may or may not feel equipped to develop surveys or interview questions. Consultants may help you learn and build your capabilities for the development of future needs assessments. Even if you have the expertise, do you have the software that could help you easily analyze the data after it is collected? A consulting firm may have access to these systems more readily than you.

Another issue is whether or not you have the content expertise. For example, if you do not have a strong background in finance, you may lack the knowledge to conduct an adequate needs assessment for the development of a finance course.

Timing

Do you and/or your staff have the time to do the assessment? This will depend on the requirements of the assessment and how comprehensive it needs to be, as well as your other priorities. Do you plan to use surveys? Will you interview people? Will you make observations of people performing their jobs? Will you analyze performance data?

Obviously, a request for a brown-bag lunch series on time management will require much less of you than an assessment for the development of a computerized simulation on strategy and finance. The rigor of the assessment should be matched to the need. Once you determine the requirements of the assessment, you will know whether you have the resources available in your organization. For more in-depth programs, hiring a consultant may save you significant time.

Cost

Hiring someone from the outside is more costly than doing the needs assessment yourself. Do you have the budget? Travel expenses and daily rates are issues to be considered. How many days will it take to do the assessment? If interviews need to be done in person, where are the people located? Will you or the consultants need to travel? If consultants travel, they may only be able to interview a person or two in a particular location. In all likelihood, you will need to pay for an entire day of the consultant's time, even if that consultant only spends part of the day interviewing.

Context

You or a member of your team knows your organization better than someone from the outside. You know the business, the organizational structure, culture, and job expectations. There is less for you to learn about the organization than a consultant; so depending on the problem, you might be able to save some time getting to the source of the problem.

On the other hand, you may wear blinders or be too close to the situation to see it accurately. Your biases may cause you to inaccurately assess the situation. In these cases, an external consultant who has distance from your organization might be more able to diagnose the problem and identify obstacles to a successful implementation.

Depending on the nature of the problem, some employees might feel more comfortable being open with an external consultant. They may feel less risk calling attention to problems when talking with someone from the outside. On the other hand, employees may feel threatened by an external consultant and safer with you.

Tradeoff Factors

After exploring the knockout factors, if you are not certain whether you should outsource, consider some of the associated tradeoffs.

Organizational Learning. There is important learning in the assessment phase. If you conduct the needs assessment, you will learn more about the dynamics of your organization, as well as more about your internal clients. You will understand the source of the problem you are trying to solve. This information is important as you build the solution. It is also helpful to you for future initiatives. The same is true for consultants. They will learn about your organization through the needs assessment phase. Having first-hand information about your organization will put them in a better position to design the next phases of the initiative. Be aware that, if you want your consultants involved in the design and delivery phases and you do not involve them in the assessment, they may not know your organization deeply enough to make a significant contribution later.

Networking and Influence. A needs assessment potentially puts you in contact with more people in your organization. It provides you with the opportunity to build better partnerships with your key clients and can contribute to your ability to influence others.

Good consultants should help build receptivity for solutions that may result from the assessments they do. Their goal should be to help you be successful in your organization. As experts from the outside, they may have a greater capacity than you to influence. It is not surprising to feel that you cannot be a prophet in your own land, so you may decide to let your consultants take this role.

Your Final Decision: To Insource or to Outsource

After exploring the tradeoffs, you ultimately need to decide the best way to proceed. You have three choices:

- Delegate the assessment to the consultant

- Do the assessment yourself

- Partner with the consultant and do the assessment jointly

There is no right or wrong answer regarding this decision. However, all things being equal, there can be the greatest value in establishing a true partnership for assessment. This model enables you to balance many factors, including time, resources, budget, and expertise. You can collaborate with your consultants, getting to know your organization, the source of the problem, and each other. You will be able to interpret the data jointly. Both of you will be equally knowledgeable about the problem and in a better position to determine the solution. Having a similar foundation, you will be in the best position to move forward jointly to design the subsequent initiative.

Assessment Issues

Training Director, Banking and Finance Institution

"I wanted to use more computer-based solutions. We couldn't keep up with all the requests for training, and there was pressure to reduce travel expenses. There was still quite a bit of fear of technology in certain segments of the business.

"I hired a consultant to develop our first technology-based course and asked the consultant to do a needs assessment. When I checked in with him half-way through his interviews, I realized that he was spending most of his time marketing the program and little time trying to understand the training needs and barriers to implementation. I was glad he was trying to build receptivity, but we also needed to understand the issues more fully. I knew I needed to get more personally involved."

Lesson: If you delegate the needs assessment to a consultant, it is important to review and approve the plan and associated questions before beginning the work. There needs to be a balance between marketing a future program and obtaining needed information for program design.

Seeds of an effective training program are planted in a high-quality needs assessment. Thoroughly discuss the plan for the assessment and then stay close enough to the project to ensure you get the results you need. The above story points to three important issues to consider when outsourcing your assessment:

- Access
- Buy-in
- Methodology

Access

In planning the assessment, determine who the consultants will need to interview or survey. You will want to take into consideration factors such as:

- Who has the knowledge?
- Where does sponsorship need to be built?
- How many people is it necessary to interview or survey?

Then pave the way to these internal resources. Return to Chapter 8 on positioning consultants in your organization. You will find a discussion of some of the best ways to prepare people for the project and their involvement with your consulting partners. If there are other aspects of the needs assessment, such as observing business processes or reviewing relevant data, help the consultants gain needed access.

Check to be sure that the consultants are getting the cooperation and information that they need. You may need to run some interference from time to time, since they are not known in your organization.

Buy-In

The needs assessment phase has two major functions:

- To analyze the problem
- To build support and receptivity to the solution

Consultants report that many training managers focus more on the former and spend insufficient time and energy on the latter. There is a delicate balance that must be maintained. You want to conduct an objective assessment, gathering accurate and meaningful data that will help you design the best solution. However, you also want to use this phase of the work to market and gain support for the initiative. Discuss these issues directly with your consulting partners as you plan the assessment. In the above story, the consultant went too far selling his program and did not dig deeply enough into organizational issues to understand barriers to an effective implementation.

Make sure building program receptivity is balanced with the need to get information that will be useful for the program design. A good way to handle this dilemma is to follow the guidance of Steven Covey as expressed in his book, *The 7 Habits of Highly Effective People*. Seek first to understand, then to be understood. Ask questions first. Understand the issues related to your initiative. Once you understand the perspective of the people you or your consultants are interviewing, then you can help them see the benefits of your intervention (Covey, 1989).

Methodology

In planning with your consulting partners, explore the methodology you will use to gather data. You will balance issues such as budget, available time, and the need to build support. For example, you may feel that a large quantity of data is required to do an accurate analysis, and you may have a limited budget. You might, therefore, consider an efficiency model, such as a survey. However, you will also need to consider the impact of a large number of people receiving a survey when a change is afoot. Receiving a survey with a limited explanation might cause unnecessary anxiety in the organization. You may decide that a more personal touch is required to help sell the initiative in your organization. Therefore, you might choose interviews or focus groups as your approach.

Be sure to review surveys or interview questions. Consultants may present these to you or you may jointly develop them. Make sure you are comfortable with the questions and avoid biases as much as possible.

If You Do Not Involve the Consultant

Many organizations do their own assessments and call in a consultant once this initial phase is complete. If consultants are not involved until a later phase, they will not have first-hand experience in your organization. This lack of direct contact may make it more difficult for them to grasp the problems, understand the culture, and get a sense of the needs of the target population. Sometimes it can be difficult for the training manager to translate this information to consultants. The result can be that the consultants make recommendations based on inadequate information, or they appear too theoretical when they engage with employees at a later point.

If you decide to conduct the needs assessment yourself, recognize that your consultant will need to understand the findings thoroughly. The worksheet in Exhibit 11.1, Needs Assessment Findings, can help you communicate what you learn in the assessment to your consulting partners

Even if you conduct the assessment yourself, you may decide that there is value in giving the consultant some direct contact with your employees after sharing the results. You might invite the consultants to spend a day or two in your organization meeting key personnel to get a better sense of the culture and validate the findings of the assessment.

Partnership Update

After completing the assessment phase of the project, conduct another partnership update. This is a good opportunity to stop action and evaluate your progress on the project and the effectiveness of your partnership. It is also

Exhibit 11.1. Needs Assessment Findings.

Instructions: Provide the results of your needs assessment to your consulting partners. Use the following table to record what you have learned.

Project: _____

1. Background of request	
2. Project sponsor(s)	
3. Link to organization strategy	
4. Link to associated initiatives	
5. Description of target population (Attach job descriptions)	
6. Causes of poor performance	
7. Measures of project success	
8. Purpose of the work	
9. Requirements of intervention	
10. Timing issues	
11. Previous relevant initiatives	
12. Resistance (people/departments)	
13. Subject-matter experts	
14. Other	

important to think about next steps and what is needed in the partnership going forward. Consider the following:

- Are you and your consultants making the progress you had hoped to make?

- How is the partnership evolving?

- Are you beginning to feel comfortable and confident with each other?

- Are there ways to improve your working relationship?

Exhibit 11.2, The Partnership Update for assessment, may be a useful tool as you plan for this meeting.

If you are using the formal approach for the partnership update, complete the Partnership Scorecard again. It can be found in Chapter 9. Ask your consulting partners to do the same in advance of your meeting. Use the scorecard to guide your discussion. Compare your ratings and comments with those from your last partnership update. What progress has been made? What are issues that still need to be resolved? What new issues have surfaced?

If you are using a less formal approach, the Partnership Scorecard will not be necessary. Instead, make some notes regarding the project and the partnership. Refer back to the criteria for a successful partnership that you established in the kick-off meeting. Evaluate yourself and your consulting partners against these criteria. Consider what is working and where improvements are needed.

Meet for the partnership update. Compare your perspectives. Highlight progress and improvements. Be sure to seek feedback on yourself and your team. Consider the following questions:

- Given the challenges we are facing, what could we do to make the project more successful?

- What could my team and I do to become better partners?

Be open to feedback. Identify and document goals for the remainder of the project.

Exhibit 11.2. Partnership Update: Assessment of Need.

Instructions: This worksheet can help you plan the partnership update that follows the assessment phase of your project. It provides you with questions that you might want to explore with your consulting partners. This worksheet can be used in association with the Service Partnership Scorecard (Exhibit 9.4). Use the notes column on the right to prepare for the discussion. Document suggestions for improvement or agreements at the bottom of the page and bring these notes to future partnership updates.

Project: _____

Questions for Discussion	Notes
How would you rate the effectiveness of our assessment? • Do we have the data that we need to move forward? • What might be missing?	
How would you rate the effectiveness of our partnership? • If using the Service Partnership Scorecard, share ratings and comments. • If using an informal approach, rate each other against criteria for a successful partnership established at kick-off meeting.	
How well have we addressed the issues that we identified at our previous partnership update? • What improvements have we made? • What opportunities do we still have for the future?	
Given the challenges of the next phase of our work, what could we do to make the project more successful?	
What could my team and I do to become better partners?	
Agreements:	

The needs assessment phase of any project is crucial. Accurate data from the assessment phase leads to a quality design. The chapter that follows describes how best to work with your consulting partners through the design and development phases of a project.

■ ■ ■ ■

Key Ideas

- The most skilled training managers approach their work as performance consultants. They use the assessment phase of a project to determine the underlying causes of poor performance. They avoid using training as a quick fix.

- The following knockout factors and associated tradeoff factors will influence whether or not you decide to outsource the needs assessment phase of a project:

  - Knockout factors

    - Expertise

    - Timing

    - Cost

    - Context

  - Tradeoff factors

    - Organizational learning

    - Networking and influence

- Involving consultants in the needs assessment phase of projects gives them first-hand information about your organization. This information can enable them to build a better solution.

- If you outsource a needs assessment, stay close to the project. Help to determine the goals of the assessment and jointly plan the approach with your consulting partners.

- There are three important issues to consider when outsourcing your assessment:

  - Access

  - Buy-in

  - Methodology

- If you choose not to outsource the assessment, make sure you fully clarify the findings with your consultants, who may be involved in a later phase of the initiative.

- End the assessment phase by conducting a partnership update with your consulting partners. The update will help you learn to work more effectively together in the future.

Design and Development

Vice President, Learning and Development, Insurance Company

"I worked with a consulting firm on a senior leadership training program over a period of four years. Each year the program received positive feedback. Now we were facing a merger that would double our size. Suddenly the program, which was scheduled to run again in three months, no longer seemed sophisticated enough. Our partnership paid off. We quickly reassessed the needs, rewrote objectives, and put together a new design to make it more challenging and provocative.

"While the consultants developed the content, I conducted conference calls with participants, supervisors, and HR executives to re-establish expectations. I also took the new approach to key stakeholders for feedback.

"We worked in tandem until the program launch. If you saw us working together, it would have been difficult to tell who was external and who was internal. We rolled up our sleeves, knew each other's strengths, and worked as a team to create the new program."

Lesson: Some of your best results can come from full collaboration on design and development. Your consulting partners can help ensure that programs that run over multiple years stay fresh in light of changes in the business.

Benefits of Outsourcing Design and Development

Training managers frequently rely on outside expertise for design and development of training. With limited staffs, training managers must use resources wisely and spend their time where they will get the best return. They, therefore, focus their efforts on the most strategic aspects of the job, such as setting strategy, working with senior leaders to position training properly, diagnosing organizational problems, and overseeing the quality of training. Development of training is often viewed as less strategic work because it is time-consuming and detail-oriented. If there is a technology-based solution, it can also require specific skills that the training department may not possess.

If you outsource the design and development of training, it is important to maintain strong partnerships with consultants to be sure programs meet the needs of your organization and are delivered on time and on budget. You are in a pivotal position and must ensure alignment between the consultants and your organization. They must design and develop instruction that is aligned to the mission, philosophy, and culture of your organization. Their programs must enable your participants to perform according to stated objectives. While they develop programs, your role is to build support and receptivity for those programs.

This chapter outlines the elements of the design and development phases, explores how resources can be allocated between the training department and external consultants, and then describes ways of working collaboratively to ensure a quality product. The chapter ends with pitfalls to avoid during design and development.

Outputs of the Design and Development Phases

Before looking at how you can work with consultants through the design and development phases of a project, it is best to understand the outputs of each phase. Knowing what needs to be done will help you determine who can best do the job.

Design Phase Outputs

The data gathered during the assessment phase is the source of the overall design for your training initiative. Your design is basically your plan. Its output is usually a document that includes a description of the following:

- Background with a summary of the findings of the assessment phase

- Description of the target population

- Overall objectives of the program

- Description of what will not be included in the training

- Class size

- Description of pre-course assignments and activities

- Description of each module of instruction including

  - Learning objectives

  - Instructional treatment

  - Means of measurement

- Plan for follow-up after the training to ensure sustainability

  - What participants will be expected to do

  - How management will support and reinforce the training

- Plan for program pilot

- Plan for evaluating participant learning and the impact of the training

  - If technology-based, what will be a passing score

  - If classroom training, how you will know whether participants have met the objectives of the program

- How you will obtain participant reactions to the program

- How you will measure the ability of participants to apply what they have learned to the job

- How you will know whether the program has helped improve performance

- Implementation plan

  - Description of how you will market the program

  - Discussion of how the training will be conducted (classroom or computer-based)

  - Technology requirements if computer-based

  - Description of who will deliver the program if classroom-based and his or her qualifications

  - Description of where the training will be delivered

  - A schedule for implementation

  - Required management support and reinforcement

- Required supplies and collateral

The Program Design worksheet in Exhibit 12.1 is a template you and your consulting partners can use to design your program. It contains the elements of a training design.

Development Phase Outputs

The development phase may include the following outputs:

- Trainer's guide

- Participant materials

- Materials for managers that will help them support the training

- Handouts, including assessments, pre-course materials, role plays, and exercises

- Materials for program evaluations

Exhibit 12.1. Program Design.

Instructions: You and your consulting partners can use this template to design your training program.

Project: _____

Design Elements	Description
Background/summary of needs assessment	
Target population	
Program objectives	
What is not included in training?	
Class size	
Pre-course assignments	
Description of each module • Learning objectives • Instructional treatment • Means of measurement	
Follow-up activities to ensure application to the job • Development plans • Expectations for supervisors	
Plan for program pilot	
Plan to evaluate participant learning	
Plan to evaluate program effectiveness • Participant reaction • Behavior change on the job • Impact on the business	
Implementation plan • Marketing plans • Schedule for training • Who will deliver/where • Requirements, if technology-based	
Supplies/collateral required	

- Materials for follow-up studies to measure the impact of the program

- Marketing materials and announcements for the program, including logistical arrangements

- If technology-based, directions to access the program

How to Involve Consultants During Design and Development

Now that the elements of the design and development phase are clear, you can examine the question of who will do the work on these phases. As in the assessment phase, there are many ways to approach the partnership. You can delegate the majority of the work to the consultant, it can be a shared responsibility, or you can do all of the design and development work and hire the consultant for implementation. The factors such as expertise, timing, cost, context, and the opportunity for learning that were outlined in the assessment section are the same issues to consider as you decide how to allocate resources to complete these phases of the project. The Strategic Sourcing Decision Model found in Chapter 3 will help you make the decision. Decision tradeoffs are described below.

Be aware that the more knowledgeable you are about course design and development, the better partner you will be as you outsource these functions. If you have experience in course design, you will be able to provide better input and feedback, and you will feel more comfortable doing so. You will have a better sense of the types of educational activities that are required to ensure learning. It is more likely that you will know whether or not a lesson is the proper level for the audience. If you do not have a strong background in course design, enroll in a course on how to develop instruction or challenge yourself to develop a program for your organization. These kinds of experiences will help you gain self-confidence.

If you are working on technology-based programs, it is crucial to stay abreast of technological advancements in the field. By attending conferences and reading trade journals, you will gradually learn enough to know what will and what will not work on your network. You will develop a better sense of authoring languages, issues of compatibility, the cost of instruction, and the timing that is needed for development. You will also meet colleagues and potential vendors who can help guide you as you are developing greater expertise in the area of technology-based training.

Delegate Design and Development to the Consultant

You may decide to delegate the design and development of a program to a consultant. The program may be completely customized or an off-the-shelf program that is customized for the organization. Fully outsourcing the development of a new program is usually the most expensive option available to the training manager.

Even if a program is fully outsourced, the training manager retains responsibility to manage the project. Project management includes providing direction on the program design, ensuring access to subject-matter experts, planning for the implementation, and giving feedback at regular intervals to be sure that the project stays on track and meets requirements. Many a project has gotten off track because a training manager did not take the time to work in partnership with the consultants on these issues.

How should the training manager be involved? Training managers may schedule meetings with consultants to provide input on content or approach. Consultants may present alternatives and ask the training manager for feedback on what might work best. In cases of technology-based course development, it is especially important for training managers to have direct contact with the people who do the work to provide direction on design, color, and look and feel. Designers often provide samples to which the training manager responds. The proper look and feel can make a difference to audience receptivity. Input on casework is also important so that the program seems realistic to the end user.

Share Responsibility for Design and Development with the Consultant

In this model, the training manager and the consultant share responsibility for design and development of a program. This approach takes significant time and involvement on the part of the training manager and assumes the training manager has course development expertise. The model calls for frequent, and often lengthy, meetings in which ideas are reviewed and challenged. Usually, the team jointly develops the overall design of the program. Once these have been confirmed, they divide the responsibility for course development, with each of the team members taking responsibility for some portion of the program. Another version of this model is to have the team jointly build the design of the program, and then have the consultants do the course development. As segments of instruction are completed, the entire team reviews materials and provides feedback to the team member responsible for that portion of the development. Because this approach to development is shared, it can be a less expensive option than fully outsourcing the project.

Most training managers and consultants agree that the greater the partnership, the greater the effectiveness of the program. However, a shared approach to design and development takes a training manager and consultant who both have self-confidence. They must be able to admit when they do not know something, ask for help, challenge each other's thinking, and be open to feedback. The partnership benefits from the expertise of the internal, who knows the organization best, and the external, who brings new knowledge to the design and development process. Given the synergistic nature of partnerships, this approach also has the potential for the greatest creativity.

Design and Develop In-House, Hire Consultants for Implementation

Designing and developing a program by members of the training department is the least expensive approach to creating a new training program, but the most time-consuming. It requires internal course development expertise. Once the program design is complete, the training manager may choose to hire consultants or trainers from the outside for delivery. Many consultants find this work the least fulfilling, because they do not have creative input to the design and development of the program. It can be difficult to deliver someone else's program. Consultants in this situation sometimes describe themselves as "an extra pair of hands." On the other hand, there are consultants who do not have program design skills and prefer delivery.

How to Maintain Partnerships with Consultants During Design and Development

Regardless of how you utilize consultants, you will want to ensure positive working relationships. You will also want to stay involved sufficiently to get the desired results. This section examines ways of working with consultants through design and development that ensure that objectives are achieved and strong partnerships are maintained.

Communicate Regularly

Regular communication is a best practice in successful partnerships and in successful projects. Stay in regular contact with the consultants to understand how the project is progressing. Frequent checks give you the opportunity to offer suggestions, provide feedback, and help deal with obstacles that may occur. Do not assume everything is fine unless you hear it from the consultants. Do not wait to communicate until it is time to review program materials. You may be able to catch problems early and respond to them before they become too serious. It is useful to put regular meeting times on the calendar for the duration of the project. The following questions may guide your discussions:

- How is the work progressing?
- What issues have surfaced since our last contact?
- Are you gaining access to subject-matter experts in the organization as needed?
- Do we seem to be on track for our next scheduled review of materials?
- Are we staying within our budget, or are there concerns about the budget?
- What can I do to better support you?

Notice that the questions are designed to continue building the partnership. Both parties are responsible for project success. You want to know how the work is progressing. You also want to let the consultants know you are available for support.

Vice President, Learning and Development, Financial Services

"I wanted to use learning maps, the large visual aids that help you have conversations about strategies and business processes. Our climate is very formal. How things look is important. Learning maps often have cartoon-like figures, and I knew that wouldn't work for us. I sent samples of our annual report and other brochures to give the graphic designer a sense of what we needed. He just couldn't do it. I must have reviewed the maps three times, and the characters were still cartoon-like. The graphic designer got angry. I talked it over with the account executive. Eventually I had to escalate it to the president of the firm. It helped us get what we needed."

Lesson: There will be times when you need to escalate problems on a project involving consultants. Be assertive and confront these situations with respect for the people involved.

It is not uncommon to find it necessary to challenge some aspect of a project during the development phase. Confronting a situation early is a best practice and avoids added cost for revisions down the road. If you are dissatisfied with some aspect of a project, discuss the issue with the person who is responsible. If you cannot resolve the issue, let the person know that you plan to discuss the problem with the project manager, account executive, or other appropriate party. It is best to avoid surprises. As in the example of the conflict over the learning map, be sensitive when dealing with programs that have significant graphical treatment. In such cases, you are basically dealing with artists and their artwork. Training managers who are successful in these negotiations indicate the need to be particularly sensitive when working with creative people. Keep in mind, you are always trying to balance your outcome with the relationship. Chapter 16, on managing conflict, will give you ideas on how best to confront difficult situations.

Take Calculated Risk

You may have to take some risks in the design and development phase of a project.

Independent Consultant

"I was hired by a public utility. The industry was facing deregulation and competition for the first time in its history. Senior leadership believed that a shift in the culture was required for future success. I met with a senior leader in human resources to review plans for an upcoming intervention. He seemed satisfied with the approach and in a very serious tone said, 'This is fine. Let's just make sure we don't change too much around here.' It was hard to avoid laughing."

Lesson: Be willing to take risks and be open to innovative approaches.

The story of the HR executive who did not want too much change in his culture change initiative is an extreme and amusing case. The work of training and development is all about change. Why introduce a training or organization development initiative if you are not expecting change? Change involves risk. What level of risk are you willing to take when you invite a consultant into your organization? Of course, in some organizations, just inviting a consultant into the organization is a risk.

Many consultants indicate that training managers are often unwilling to take risks. They are typically cautious and conservative and respond to suggestions by saying, "That wouldn't work around here." Such a remark might mask fear on the part of the training manager. Consultants question why they have been brought into an organization if the goal is to repeat the same kinds of initiatives that have been done previously and have not yet produced the desired outcomes. After all, part of the reason you hire consultants is to get fresh ideas.

How open are you to innovative solutions? Would you try something new and potentially more provocative than usual? Are you willing to set up experiences that might cause your organization members to have conversations that they typically do not have? Are you willing to try a technology-based solution in an environment that has been fearful of technology because it is best for the organization in the long term? These are some of the issues to be considered during the design and development phase of a project.

Consultants often challenge your thinking and push you beyond your comfort zone. In the end, you have to determine what level of risk is appropriate for you and your organization. You are more of an expert on the culture and the various players than the consultants are.

Training managers often grow into their willingness to take risk. They begin with more conservative approaches, but once they have established strong reputations they are more likely to venture out. If you are ready to step out, you will want to partner closely with your consultants to minimize unnecessary risk.

Ensure Cultural Fit

How do you get a truly customized design that fits your culture? The following may be helpful:

- Begin by being very clear about program objectives

- Provide your consultants with access to leaders and content experts

- Make sure consultants are clear about how the program links to strategic objectives

- Help consultants link the training to what is happening in the organization

- Stay focused on the level of the participants and their concerns

- Communicate what is important for training to be successful

  - Requirements for pace

  - The kinds of experiences both in content and methodology that people have had previously and what has worked and not worked

  - Language or jargon that might help or hinder

- Stay close to the project and regularly provide feedback

- If you do not feel comfortable that you are the best person to provide feedback, ask others in your organization to help

Take a Stand on Content

Although important for all projects, it is especially important for training managers to help consultants who are developing technology-based programs determine the program content. With the help of subject-matter experts, the objectives and content should be clarified on the front end of a project. It is sometimes difficult to finalize content because training programs are often developed concurrently with associated new business processes and systems. Although difficult to do, training managers should try to put a stake in the ground after which no changes can be made unless they are deemed mission critical. Constant changes in content are costly and time-consuming. Another approach, if you are working on leading-edge content, is to build greater flexibility into the contract price to allow for more creativity and change.

Remove Obstacles

As training manager, your role is to help remove obstacles that may prevent your consultants from being successful. Typical obstacles that can surface include handling difficulty with subject-matter experts, gaining access to people in your organization, and resolving issues for which there is conflicting direction.

Working with subject-matter experts can be challenging. They may not have as much time for the project as might be needed. They may also expect you to include more information in training programs than the participants actually need. The best way to engage subject-matter experts is to negotiate the time needed from them at the beginning of a project. However, even if you gain their support in the beginning, it may be necessary to contact them in the middle of a project and remind them of the importance of their involvement. If they cannot give you the time your consultants need, you may need to identify additional resources. You may also have to negotiate with them regarding how much technical information should be included in a program. Your external consultants may need your help, since you probably have a stronger relationship with the subject-matter experts than the consultants do.

Your consultants may have difficulty making contact with people in your organization. For example, they may need to interview senior leaders to get direction and information for development of casework. Perhaps they need to spend additional time with members of the IT department if the program is technology-based. Sometimes consultants are unable to get responses from people in your organization because they are busy or do not understand the importance of their involvement. Sometimes consultants are blocked because there is resistance to the initiative. Regardless of the cause, your help is needed.

Another obstacle a consultant faces is how to deal with conflicting direction. Be available to help clarify the proper direction. Sometimes consultants are in need of political information to help resolve the difficulty. Other times they will need your advice because you know the direction you want the program to take. There may also be times when you need to bring the parties together who are providing conflicting information and mediate the conflict.

Maintain a Regular Review Schedule

Launching a program that is well-received is based on building support for the program along the way. Careful review and approvals pave the way for success. At the kick-off meeting, you should have identified who needs to review the various segments of the program and how that review will take place. Reviewers may include key leaders, an advisory board, or subject-matter experts. They can help ensure that the content is accurate and that the program fits the direction and culture of the organization.

Establish a regular schedule for review and feedback without micromanaging consultants. Creative course design and development takes time. However, too loose a review schedule can cause a program to derail, potentially increase its cost, and ultimately delay delivery. Risks are greater on technology-based training projects, where revisions are often more costly than for traditional instruction in terms of time and money. Changing words on a page is much easier than reprogramming a segment of computer-based instruction.

Establish times to meet and review what has been developed when it makes sense for the given project. Training managers often negotiate review dates when segments of the program are complete. Critical checkpoints include:

- The project design
- The completion of each major segment of instruction
- Revisions on segments of instruction
- Review of the evaluation plan and associated materials

A technology-based program will include a more comprehensive review schedule. Reviews of the following are critical:

- The project design
- A content outline
- Overall look and feel of the program, including the graphical treatment
- Prototype
- Storyboards
- Scripts and screens
- Final product
- Evaluation plan and materials
- Associated training materials if it is a blended solution

Structure of the Review Process. Clarify how the review process will work including:

- When you will receive materials to review
- Who will need to be involved
- When feedback is due
- How the feedback should be given
- When you can expect to see the feedback incorporated into the program

By reviewing each segment of instruction as it is completed, you will be able to provide feedback to the consultants to ensure a successful program.

Review Criteria. In advance, determine the review criteria. The Program Review worksheet (Exhibit 12.2) can be a starting point. The consultants will probably have specific issues or aspects of the program about which they want your feedback. Be sure to ask them what kind of feedback they are seeking.

Timing for Feedback. Work out a schedule to provide feedback. When will you receive materials and when will they require your feedback? It can be frustrating to receive an email attachment the morning of a conference call in which you are scheduled to provide feedback on that document. You may not have the time to do a thorough review and may frustrate the consultants because of inadequate feedback. Avoid this problem by negotiating for sufficient time to review materials.

Once you work out a review schedule, be sure that you meet the due dates. Meeting your commitments for review helps the consultants meet their due date for the entire program. It will also enable them to manage their resources. If you do not provide your feedback in a timely manner, your consultants may be sitting with nothing to do. Then once your feedback arrives, they may not have sufficient time to meet the overall project deadline. Adhering to these schedules is especially important on technology-based projects when the vendor is coordinating numerous resources (instructional designers, graphic artists, computer programmers).

It is also important to establish a schedule in your organization for collection of feedback. If there are several reviewers, they need to know when they will receive materials and when their feedback is due. To avoid confusion, it is best to summarize all the feedback so that it goes back to the consultants through a single point of contact. Having a single point of contact ensures that you are comfortable with all the feedback. If there are discrepancies, you can work these issues out prior to providing it to the consultants.

Version Control. Since you will probably review a program more than once, it is important to control the versions and make sure that your feedback is incorporated into the program. Version control is especially important on a computer-based

Exhibit 12.2. Program Review.

Instructions: Establish criteria for the review of a training program so that reviewers are clear about the kind of feedback you are seeking. You and your consulting partners can use this template as a starting point to establish criteria for the review. Add or delete criteria as appropriate.

Project/Module: _____

Reviewer: _____

Review Criteria	Reviewer Feedback/Recommendations
Does it meet stated objectives?	
Is it linked to company objectives?	
Does it fit the culture?	
Does it align with other programs?	
Is level appropriate to target audience?	
Are examples realistic?	
Is there enough variation to maintain interest?	
Is there sufficient interaction?	
Are materials engaging?	
Does it fit with overall design?	
Are there appropriate transitions?	
Are materials free of spelling and grammatical errors?	
Does the content meet legal standards?	

project, which typically has many more details. Either you or someone from your team should control the review and feedback process. It is particularly helpful if this individual is very detail-oriented. Ask your consultants to date each version, so that you can keep track of revisions. After a review, feedback should be summarized either online or in writing and sent to the consultants. A copy should be made for your organization and can be used at a later point to check that changes have been made. Have a follow-up conversation to explain the feedback so that it is fully understood. Then clarify when the feedback will be incorporated and returned to you. At that point, either you or a member of your team can do a final check.

Manage Scope Creep

Training Manager, Health Care Agency

"While brainstorming the design of a leadership program, we thought it might be a good idea to add executive coaching to the program. We knew this addition would help ensure better long-term results. The consulting firm was willing to help, but indicated that it was a change in project scope. Feeling that it was a worthwhile investment, we decided to renegotiate the contract."

Lesson: Be aware of scope creep when working with consultants and readjust the contract to accommodate significant changes in scope.

During the design or development phase, it is not uncommon for the scope of a project to increase. A creative solution that you did not anticipate suddenly surfaces. Refer to Chapter 10 on project management for an additional discussion of scope creep.

Most consultants are willing to do some extras on a project in the name of good customer service and generosity of spirit. They want to support you and build a long-term relationship. It is, however, unrealistic to expect them to take on significantly more on a project than was originally negotiated in the contract. They expect, and greatly appreciate, a training manager who quickly acknowledges scope creep and demonstrates a willingness to renegotiate the contract. It is important at these times to recognize that your relationship is a partnership. Each of you has expectations. You want good value for your investment. The consultants are in the business to provide a service and also need to make a profit. The key to successfully renegotiating your agreement is a win-win approach.

Pilot the Program

It is risky to implement a program without testing. A pilot enables you to test your program, get feedback from participants who represent your target population, and make revisions before your official launch. Your consulting partners should participate in the pilot if they have helped you design and develop the program. With this first-hand experience, they will be in the best position to make needed revisions. The Pilot Plan worksheet (Exhibit 12.3) is a template you can use with your consulting partners to plan your pilot.

Although the pilot is a test, it is important to properly position the program to your participants. Remember, your participants are forming an impression of the program through the pilot. If the program is very rough at this point, they may have a negative reaction and word may spread to future participants. Therefore, set realistic expectations, because the program is usually not fully polished at this point. Explain to the group what kind of feedback you are seeking and how you will collect it. Allow adequate time at the end of the program to solicit overall feedback and suggestions for improvement.

It is just as important to properly position consultants in your pilot as it is to position the program. Demonstrate your partnership. Explain the consultants' backgrounds and why you selected them. You want the consultants and your participants to feel comfortable with each other so that you can get the most honest and helpful feedback. When conducting a debriefing at the end of the program, be careful that you and your consulting partners stay open. Avoid rationalizing what participants say or acting defensively. If there are negatives in the feedback at the pilot, the same negatives are likely to reappear in the implementation of the program unless you address the issues.

Exhibit 12.3. Pilot Plan.

Instructions: You and your consulting partners can use this template to plan your pilot program.

Project: _____

Considerations	Plan
Date and time	
Location	
Trainer(s)	
Participants	
Observers and their roles • Timekeeper • Record participant questions	
Means of collecting feedback • Feedback forms • Post-program debriefing Participants Observers	
Feedback you are seeking • Relevance • Clarity • Realism of examples • Pace • Length (too long or short) • Engaging • Suggestions for improvement	

On completion of the pilot, jointly determine what changes you will make before the launch of the program. Allow for a further review as you negotiate completion dates. Finally, the pilot is an important milestone, so be sure to express appreciation to your partners for their contributions.

Pitfalls

Projects can derail easily. There is the potential for missed deadlines and for the scope and budget of a project to expand beyond its original boundaries. Projects that are not well-managed can miss the mark and not achieve their objectives or end up not fitting the culture. Be aware of the following pitfalls when working with consultants through the design and development phases:

- Not staying close enough to the project to ensure its success

- Micromanaging the project to the point that creative solutions are stifled

- Developing programs based on poor performance consulting and discovering after the fact that the program had no impact because it addressed the wrong issues

- If technology-based, not including the appropriate partners from your IT department

- Not giving consultants access to subject-matter experts

- Getting insufficient feedback from key stakeholders

- Not helping the consultants understand how the program fits into the larger context

- Not conducting a pilot to test the program

- Building a timeline that does not allow sufficient time for trainers to prepare for delivery

- Not building necessary support for the program with management

Continue Partnership Updates

The partnership update can be used throughout the design and development phases to help you avoid these pitfalls. Before moving into implementation, conduct the partnership update to review progress on the project and to learn from the experience. Remember that the communication at the partnership update is on two levels—the project and the relationship. It is also a time for the team to project into the future and determine what will be needed in the implementation phase to ensure success.

Review the guidelines for the partnership update in Chapter 9. The worksheet for the partnership update for the design and development phase (Exhibit 12.4) can help you plan for the meeting. Continue the process you have previously established, using the Partnership Scorecard or a more informal approach. Regardless of the degree of formality, the following questions may guide your discussion:

- How would you evaluate the design and development phases of our project?

- What worked? What did not work? Why?

- What can we do in the future to work more effectively together?

- What will be needed in the implementation to ensure success?

- What concerns, if any, do you have about the project or our team that you may not have mentioned?

Review the notes you took at your last partnership update discussion. Share the issues with the team. Ask the group to assess how well the team has addressed the issues since the last discussion. Take notes during the discussion, especially recording any commitments team members make regarding how to strengthen the partnership in the future.

The design and development phases of a project are often the most time-consuming. Some of the activities you and your consulting partners are doing include researching topics, building learning activities, writing leaders' guides and participant materials, and reviewing materials with subject-matter experts. High-quality design and development work will pay big dividends in the

Exhibit 12.4. Partnership Update: Design and Development.

Instructions: Use this worksheet to help plan the partnership update that follows the design and development phases of your project. The worksheet provides questions you may want to explore with your consulting partners. It can be used in association with the Service Partnership Scorecard (Exhibit 9.4). Use the notes column on the right to prepare for the discussion. Document suggestions for improvement or agreements at the bottom of the page and bring these notes to future partnership updates.

Project: _____

Questions for Discussion	Notes
How would you rate the effectiveness of our program design/development? • What level of confidence do you have in the program? • What reaction are you expecting from participants?	
How would you rate the effectiveness of our partnership through design/development? • If using the Service Partnership Scorecard, share ratings and comments. • If using an informal approach, rate each other against criteria for a successful partnership established at kick-off meeting.	
How well have we addressed the issues that we identified at our previous partnership update? • What improvements have we made? • What opportunities do we still have for the future?	
Given the challenges of the next phase of our work, what could we do to make the project more successful?	
What could my team and I do to become better partners?	
Agreements:	

implementation phase of your project. Chapter 13 covers the elements of an effective implementation. It emphasizes the importance of continuing to maintain and strengthen the partnership that you have built with your consultants.

■ ■ ■ ■

Key Ideas

- Some of your best results may come from a full collaboration with external consultants on the design and development of training.

- Because the development of a training program is very detailed-oriented and viewed as less strategic work than other aspects of training (e.g., strategy development, influencing senior leaders), it is often outsourced.

- Outsourcing does not mean relinquishing responsibility. Training managers ensure programs are aligned to the mission, philosophy, and culture of the organization and that they achieve stated objectives. They build receptivity for programs while they are under development.

- Consider the following ways to involve consultants:
  - Fully delegate the design and development
  - Share responsibility for design and development
  - Design and develop internally and hire consultants to implement

- Be cautious about engaging consultants to deliver internally developed materials. Some consultants may only want to deliver their own content, while others may enjoy delivering content developed by others.

- You can maintain partnerships with consultants through design and development by:
  - Communicating regularly
  - Taking calculated risk

- Helping to determine program content

- Removing obstacles

- Maintaining a regular review and feedback schedule

- Managing scope creep

- If at all possible, pilot a new program. A pilot will enable you to test a program with less risk and make needed revisions before a program launch.

- Complete the design and development phases with a partnership update. This discussion will help you strengthen your partnership and learn how to work more effectively in the future.

13

Implementation

Lesson: Implementation requires a particular skill set. In the design phase, strategic thinking skills are important. During implementation, a detail orientation is probably more important. Enter each phase of a project anticipating the required skill set. Assess your partnership to be sure you have the proper resources to handle upcoming challenges.

Implementation is the point at which your partnership should truly pay off. The implementation is often stressful, because you are rolling out an initiative for the first time. Team members can be on edge. Everyone wants the program to go well. Tensions in the relationship between you and the consultants can distract each of you from the work and may be visible to others. If the partnership is not strong, it will have impact on quality. Continuing to support each other will help ensure success.

This chapter covers the implementation phase. It will help you maintain the partnership with consultants through the preparation for implementation, the actual implementation, and post-implementation activities.

Preparation for Implementation

As you prepare to launch your initiative, it is important to assess your relationship with the consultants and the status of the project. Then working with your consultants, build a plan to address issues to maximize your likelihood of success.

Relationship with Consultants

How is your relationship with the consultants? Have you built a strong partnership, or are there tensions below the surface? If the partnership is strong, this will serve you well during implementation. If it is not strong, it is never too late to try to improve it. Assess what is working and what is not. Consider the strengths each of you has that will be helpful in the implementation. Consider the weaknesses that could be detrimental.

Assess the State of the Project

After assessing your partnership, consider the state of your project. Are you fully confident about all aspects of the initiative? Are there aspects of the program that concern you? If so, is there anything that can be done at this point to strengthen these segments?

Meet with Consultants to Plan Implementation

Independent Training Consultant

"I arrived at the regional training location expecting to find the classroom set up and all my materials ready. I had provided directions in advance to the administrative support team. Nothing had been done, and I couldn't find anyone to help me. Participants were arriving in an hour, and significant set-up was required. I wanted to be available to meet and greet participants as they arrived. I quickly contacted the training manager by cell phone. She was able to track down a member of the administrative support team to get the room set while I greeted the participants. It was stressful, but at least the training manager was able to resolve the problem."

Lesson: Support your consulting partners by anticipating logistical needs before a program implementation. Make sure those responsible follow through to ensure a quality program.

To avoid problems, it is best to meet with consultants to plan the implementation. The Walk-Through Agenda worksheet (Exhibit 13.1) can help you plan your agenda for this meeting. Your agenda will cover items such as:

- A walk-through of the program and associated materials

- A review of the participants and any special needs they may have

- Logistical requirements

- Review of related social activities if appropriate

Exhibit 13.1. Walk-Through Agenda.

Instructions: You and your consulting partners can use this agenda as a starting point for your walk-through prior to the launch of a new program.

Project: _____

Agenda	Notes
Welcome	
Objectives for walk-through	
Review of participants	
Review of observers	
Tour of training space	
Program walk-through • Anticipated participant reaction • Logistical requirements • Requirements of evening activities • Review of materials • Supplies • AV requirements • Meal requirements	
Roles and responsibilities • Timekeeper • Note-taker	
Plans for collecting feedback	
Plans for updating during program	
Plans for partnership update after program	
Special issues	
Other	

- Discussion of roles and responsibilities at the event

- Plans for collecting feedback and evaluating the implementation

- Special issues or concerns and how to address these

Jointly look at all aspects of the implementation. Do a walk-through of the program. This meeting gives you an opportunity to discuss everything that needs to take place, what materials are needed, and who will be responsible for each aspect of the program and the associated logistics. Try to anticipate issues that may surface and determine how you will address them. Renegotiate roles and responsibilities, matching up team members to tasks based on their skills and what is needed for the implementation. Also discuss how you will collect feedback and evaluate the program. It is important to assign someone the task of timekeeping and note-taking in the program. If it is a training program, you will want to record the length of the segments of instruction, especially if you plan to repeat the program. Your note-taking should record what went well and what did not, as well as initial ideas for changes.

This meeting is a time to strengthen your relationship with the consultants and address concerns you have not previously discussed. Try to clear up any tension before the implementation. As this is a partnership and feedback should go both ways, be sure to ask for feedback from the consultants. Find out what you can do to support them in the implementation. Express your appreciation to the consultants for their contributions. Let them know that you have confidence in them and the program.

The Implementation

What differentiates a successful implementation from an unsuccessful implementation? Of course, the basics need to be in place. The program needs to be high-quality. If it is a traditional classroom-based program, the facilitators must be competent. If it is a technology-based project, the relationship with the technology group must be very strong, and the program and hardware must be fully tested. Whether classroom-based or technology-based, all logistics must be carefully planned and executed. There are three subtleties to implementation success that training managers are sometimes surprised to learn. These include:

- Establishing realistic expectations
- Positioning the program effectively
- Maintaining the partnership throughout the program

Training Manager, Transportation Company

"Years ago when I was a new training manager, I was asked to start a management development program for supervisors. Since it was high-profile, I decided to contract with a top training firm. My company had never used training consultants, and it was our first experience with management training. I was nervous about the project and my reputation. Looking back, I guess my anxiety got the better of me. I kept reminding the consultants that the program had to go well or the training department would no longer continue to get funding. I put so much pressure on them that their anxiety increased too. They probably did not perform as well as they could have. The reality was that the implementation was good and the funding continued. However, with more realistic expectations and a more relaxed approach, I think the training could have been even better."

Lesson: Set high standards for performance while maintaining realistic expectations.

Establishing Realistic Expectations

Expecting a program to go perfectly is an automatic set-up for failure. Worrying excessively that the program will go poorly is also a set-up for failure and can sometimes become a self-fulfilling prophecy. Both are extremes. Neither is helpful. A healthier attitude is that, if well-planned, a program should go well. Some aspects will go extremely well. Some aspects may not go as well and will require revisions. Discussing expectations with your consultants at the beginning of the program can take some of the pressure off and help everyone perform more effectively. In all likelihood, everyone on the team wants the program to be a success. Setting the bar high for performance is good. However, having unrealistic expectations can put too much pressure on everyone and lead to poor performance.

Positioning the Program Effectively

The beginning of your program presents an opportunity to build goodwill. This can pave the way for success, so take the beginning of your program seriously. It is a time when participants have many questions. They are wondering why they are here, how well they fit with the group, and whether or not the training will be a worthwhile investment of their time. What can you do to engage the participants, build credibility for the program, and demonstrate partnership with the consultants?

- Get everyone involved and a dialogue going as quickly as possible. Create an atmosphere that encourages participation as soon as people enter the room. Setting up an informal reception for people to meet each other before the start of the program is helpful. Make sure you and the consultants introduce yourselves to others and start to get to know the participants during the reception. The reception is not a time for last-minute review of trainer notes. If it is not appropriate to hold a reception, you and the consultants should introduce yourselves to all participants as they enter the room.

- Take formal introductions seriously. Position consultants carefully. You can introduce the consultants or they can introduce themselves. Work this out based on what is the norm for your organization or what feels most comfortable. If you introduce them, make sure participants understand who your consultants are, their backgrounds, and the value they bring to the project. Do not oversell, but be generous in your introductions and make sure your participants get a sense of the partnership you have established. Your goal is for participants to welcome the consultants into the organization in the same way you have. If the consultants introduce themselves, make sure they share their backgrounds, expertise, and perhaps something personal about themselves. Their goal should be to connect with your participants.

- Help participants see the value of the training and how they will benefit as quickly as possible. You, a senior executive, or a line manager can help make the connection between the program and the organization's strategic objectives. It is better for someone from your organization to assume this role rather than the external consultants, since they will be viewed as the outsiders and less knowledgeable about the organization's strategy. However, they can reinforce the message by sharing their industry expertise or knowledge of what other organizations are doing.

- Give people their voice in the room quickly. Create an activity in which everyone (including yourself and the consultants) has the opportunity to express themselves. With this beginning, everyone will feel more comfortable speaking up. If people do not have this opportunity early in the program, they often do not express themselves publicly at all. Make sure diverse points of view are accepted. Your goal is to make the room a safe place for people to explore new ideas. By providing an opportunity for the consultants to work with participants early in the program, you are helping them become more a part of the group. If there are multiple consultants, provide this opportunity to all of them.

Maintaining the Partnership Throughout the Program

Because the stress level can be high at this point, there is extra strain on the partnership. There are several things you can do to maintain the partnership throughout the program.

- Reflect the value you place on the partnership in the assignment of trainers. Consider balance in the assignments of trainers when internal staff members facilitate with consultants. If you want to position yourself or a member of your staff as a facilitator equal in expertise to the consultants, then be sure to give similar exposure to internal and external members of the team as you make training assignments. Maintaining balance in training assignments is also important if there are multiple consultants who have similar roles. You will want the participants to see all consultants as experts. If one is assigned significantly more to do than another, the participants may see that consultant as the more skilled facilitator. Of course, there may be instances in which a consultant has significantly less contact with participants due to the role or expertise of that individual on the project. An example might be if you bring in an industry expert for a two-hour briefing to the group as part of a larger program.

- Maintain open lines of communication, especially in the implementation phase. If an aspect of the program is not going well, either you or your consultants may decide to make an adjustment. Make sure everyone understands that all changes need to be discussed and agreed on by the entire team. It is important to include everyone's perspective to be sure changes make sense and support program objectives. Everyone also needs to be involved because a change in one portion of the program may impact another.

- Take special care when providing constructive feedback to consultants in the middle of a program. It will probably not be the first time you are providing feedback to consultants if you have been working together for a long time on a project. However, it can be a particularly stressful time. It is a rare individual who can take feedback and make an adjustment in the moment. Choose the time you give feedback carefully. It should be a time when the individual is open and can respond to what you are saying. Keep respect for the individual and the partnership foremost in your mind. If the program is not going well, the pressure you are under may cause you to blame the consultants. They may feel defensive. As with any good feedback process, let the person know what your concern is and the impact it is having. Explore the situation and jointly determine how to resolve it. Ask how you can support the individual.

Vice President, Organization Development and Training, Financial Services

"I didn't time my feedback well. I hired several consultants to support a major organizational change. We held large conferences where consultants facilitated workshops on culture change. I observed one of the consultants and felt her training style was demeaning. On the first break of the morning, I gave her some feedback. I was upset and had limited time, so my feedback was too harsh. I caught the consultant off guard, and we didn't have much time to talk about it. I just wanted her to fix the problem. After the break, the consultant's anxiety increased and her performance became even worse. I probably did need to say something at that point, but clearly my stress level interfered."

Lesson: Treat your consulting partners with respect when you provide feedback. Time the feedback carefully so there is an opportunity to have a meaningful discussion. Inappropriately timed feedback can be damaging to the individual and to the program.

Post-Implementation Activities

Your training initiative may be a one-time event or have numerous sessions implemented over time. In either case, you probably want to learn as much as you can from the experience. Although you and the team may be exhausted, take the opportunity to conduct another partnership update while the event is still fresh in your mind. If you wait, you may miss some important learning. You will probably want to do a more comprehensive evaluation at a later date. Keep in mind that this is a time for celebration. Do not miss this opportunity.

Partnership Update

This partnership update will be somewhat different from previous ones. The Partnership Update for implementation (Exhibit 13.2) and the following agenda can guide you through this meeting.

- Thank everyone for their participation and hard work.

- Review the initial feedback from the program evaluations.

- Identify what went especially well in the program.

- Identify areas that did not go as well.

- Highlight how you would change things if you were to do the program again.

- Seek feedback on the effectiveness of the partnership through the implementation phase.

- Seek feedback from consultants about your organization.

- Determine next steps as appropriate to the project.

In the partnership update, thank the consultants and members of your team for their involvement. Too often there is a tendency to highlight the problems that need to be fixed. Instead, take time to celebrate the successes. Given all the preparation and work to build the partnership, there are certainly positives to highlight.

As you review the end-of-course evaluations, look for themes. Be careful not to focus on the single comments. It is not uncommon to get conflicting feedback. Certain participants really like something, while others reject it. It is your job, along with the consultants, to determine how to resolve these issues. Acknowledge what you have learned. You may brainstorm ideas to address concerns, but avoid fixing problems now. With some time and distance, you may consider other options.

Try to be aware that people may feel sensitive at this point. A segment of instruction may have received negative feedback due to program design, the delivery, or a combination of both. The person who delivered this segment may feel vulnerable. Be supportive as you review this feedback.

Determine next steps. If you are going to conduct the program again, there may be revisions. Develop a preliminary plan for how to accomplish these. It is probably best to schedule another meeting to address these issues at a time when people are refreshed and can think more clearly and creatively.

Exhibit 13.2. Partnership Update: Implementation.

Instructions: Use this worksheet to help you plan the partnership update that follows the program implementation. This worksheet can be used in association with the Service Partnership Scorecard (Exhibit 9.4). Use the notes column on the right to prepare for the discussion. Document suggestions for improvement or agreements at the bottom of the page and bring these notes to future partnership updates.

Project: _____

Agenda	Notes
Express appreciation to the team	
Review program evaluations	
Identify program strengths	
Identify program weaknesses	
Brainstorm revisions to the program	
Seek feedback on the organization	
Seek feedback on the effectiveness of the partnership during implementation	
Determine next steps	
Agreements:	

After a program implementation, consultants usually share observations with you about the participants and your organization. They may feel that participants were engaged in the program and may have confidence that people will go back to the job and apply what they have learned. They may identify participants who demonstrated leadership potential. On the other hand, participants may have revealed information that points to lack of management support. Participants may have voiced concerns and have been unsure why they attended the program. They may be worried that they will not be able to use the skills that were taught. This information can be helpful as you work with management to ensure follow-up and application to the job. It can also help you plan future initiatives.

Celebration

You have all worked very hard on this initiative. It is time to celebrate the program and the partnership. The kind of celebration you choose is dependent on the culture of your organization and the people involved. There are many possibilities. A warm thank you, a champagne toast, a recognition luncheon, or a small gift to team members are some ways to celebrate. Your partners will appreciate the gesture.

You and your consulting partners probably have some sense of the impact your program has had on participants, based on your observations during the implementation phase. You may want to do a comprehensive evaluation of the initiative to measure its impact. Chapter 14, Evaluation, clarifies approaches you and your consulting partners can take to evaluate your program.

■ ■ ■ ■

Key Ideas

- A successful implementation requires a detail orientation. Assess your partnership to be sure you have the proper resources with the appropriate skill sets in place to handle the implementation.

- Assess the state of the partnership and the project before implementation. Identify opportunities for improvement and address these before implementation.

- Meet with your consulting partners before an implementation to do a walk-through of the program. This meeting will help you plan all details associated with the program and anticipate what is needed to ensure its success. It also provides a platform to address any issues in the relationship that might interfere with the implementation.

- A successful implementation is based on a quality program that is well executed. Attention to the following issues will contribute to success:

  - Establish realistic expectations

  - Position the program effectively

  - Maintain the partnership throughout the program

- Conduct a partnership update at the end of the implementation phase.

- Celebrate the success of the implementation.

14

Evaluation

Training Director, Large Paper Manufacturing Company

"I've never been much of a fan of training evaluation, even though everyone in the field keeps talking about its importance. I've done evaluations over the years, but management has never been particularly impressed. It's probably not my strong suit. I decided this time that, if I was going to evaluate a program, I was going to do it right. I hired an expert to help evaluate a program for high-potential buyers. What a difference it made. I discovered the importance of getting our sponsor involved on the front end. The rigorous approach that the consultant used in the development of our questions and the analysis of our results made me feel more confident. I was able to be much more convincing when I presented our findings to management. We saw an improvement in performance, and we also learned about parts of the program that needed to be strengthened. It was a great investment, and I'm glad we did it."

Lesson: Rigorous evaluation can help organizations understand the impact of training on performance. It can also help build credibility for the training department. Through their partnership, training managers and consultants can collaborate to ensure quality and a return on their investment in training.

Importance of Evaluation

Evaluation is becoming increasingly important as a means of demonstrating the value of training to management. As outsourcing increases, the need to demonstrate a return increases, especially when the rationale for outsourcing is cost savings. Even if cost savings is not the goal, evaluation needs to become a priority. Training should be run like a business, and measurement can help to ensure return on investment.

An interesting phenomenon of evaluation work is that often the follow-up process not only helps the organization understand training's impact but also helps increase results over time. For example, if an evaluation includes follow-up interviews with managers of participants to determine behavior change, interviews may remind them of the importance of ongoing coaching after the program. Evaluation studies also provide feedback to managers on the quality of their training initiatives, so that they can strengthen programs over time.

Of all aspects of training, evaluation gets the least attention by training managers. They often avoid it because of lack of expertise. There are also limited resources. When one program finishes, it is time to begin another. Consultants with expertise in evaluation can help overcome obstacles, so you can successfully evaluate training programs and demonstrate the impact of training on your organization.

Evaluation Models

The most widely recognized model for training evaluation was developed by Donald Kirkpatrick (1994). His model includes four levels: reaction, learning, behavior, and results.

Reaction

In a level one evaluation, the goal is to understand the level of satisfaction of the participants. How did the participants feel about the training? Did they find it valuable? What were their reactions to the facilitators? Were they satisfied with the learning environment? Do they think they will be able to apply what they learned back on the job? Participants typically complete questionnaires at the end of a training program to provide level one feedback. Exhibit 14.1 is a typical level one evaluation. Jack Phillips and Ron Stone (2002), in their book *How to Measure Training Results,* provide additional samples of questionnaires that can be used for level one evaluation. Today's level one evaluations frequently ask participants questions about how they plan to use the skills they have learned. Questions of this nature reinforce the importance of participants applying what they have learned back on the job.

Level one evaluation can be helpful in getting feedback on consultants you may have engaged to facilitate training programs. As a good partner, be sure your consultants are aware that you plan to use an end-of-course evaluation. Make sure they see it in advance so they understand what you plan to measure, and be sure to review the data with them at the end of the program.

Learning

A level two evaluation helps you understand whether or not participants learned what was intended in the program. The vehicle for measuring learning should be based on the objectives of the program. Testing, role plays, case studies, and simulations are often used to measure what participants learned in the program. Your consulting partners can be helpful in designing these evaluation tools.

Behavior

Measurement at the third level helps determine whether or not participants' behavior has changed when they return to the job. Have they been able to apply what they have learned, and has their performance actually improved? Level three evaluations are often done several weeks/months after participants have attended a program. Measurement may include statistical comparisons or observations of performance before and after training by supervisors, peers, and direct reports.

Exhibit 14.1. Sample End-of-Course Evaluation.

Date: _____ Your Position: _____

Title of Course: _____ Length of Time in Job: _____

Facilitator: _____

The Training Department strives to improve the quality of our programs. Please take a few moments to provide feedback by completing the following evaluation. On the line provided, fill in the number that best describes your rating for each statement using the following scale:

Strongly Disagree	Disagree	Agree	Strongly Agree
1	2	3	4

Course Design and Materials

1. The course objectives were clear. _____   4. The course materials were useful. ___

2. The content was relevant to my job. _____ 5. The course held my interest. _____

3. I can apply skills learned to my job. _____ 6. I would recommend this course to others. _____

7. What do you plan to do differently as a result of attending this program?

_____

_____

8. What may keep you from applying what you learned to the job?

_____

_____

9. What suggestions would you make to improve the effectiveness of this program?

_____

_____

Facilitator(s)   **Name:**   _____   _____

10. The instructor(s) was knowledgeable.   _____   _____

11. The instructor(s) demonstrated professional   _____   _____
    presentation skills.

12. The instructor(s) encouraged interaction.   _____   _____

13. The instructor(s) used time effectively.   _____   _____

Some programs have action-planning components to encourage participants to apply what they have learned. Participants are asked to set improvement goals at the end of training, and trainers conduct follow-up studies to determine how well the plans have been implemented and what results have been achieved.

The Fort Hill Company (www.ifollowthrough.com) offers web-based tools to help participants develop action plans. In Fort Hill's Friday5's program, participants set goals for improved performance, receive online reminders, and update progress on their action plans. Fort Hill also helps organizations measure the business impact of these plans.

As part of training, many organizations contract with outside providers to enable participants to complete 360-degree surveys of their leadership capabilities. After the program, participants select three to five items for improvement. Then several months later, their organizations help them conduct a mini 360-degree survey that provides feedback on just these items. The individual can see whether or not he or she has made progress.

Results

Level four evaluations seek to measure organizational results or business impact. Data is collected to determine improvements in areas such as sales, cost savings, error reduction, retention, and employee morale. Phillips and Stone (2002) describe a fifth level of evaluation, called return on investment. It compares the financial benefits of a program to the cost of that program. Considering the many factors that impact performance, it is complex to measure levels four and five. You may want to seek the advice of a consultant who specializes in evaluation to help you. In addition to the references already mentioned in this chapter, you may want to refer to *Bottom-Line Organization Development: Implementing & Evaluating Strategic Change for Lasting Value* by Merrill Anderson (2003).

Planning Evaluations

If you wait until the end of a program to determine how you will measure its impact, it is too late. As discussed in Chapter 9 on launching the project, the time to plan the evaluation is at the beginning of a project. It is at this point that you ask the question, "When this project is complete, how will we know whether we were successful?" Planning for the evaluation at the beginning of the project brings clarity to the program design. Often your plans for evaluation impact follow-up.

How much evaluation should you do? It all depends. You have many priorities and limited resources, so you have to determine whether or not a particular program merits a comprehensive evaluation. The more extensive your evaluation, the more it will cost in time and money. Yet, if you can demonstrate significant improvements in performance, you may get greater support for future training initiatives.

When determining the extent of your evaluation, consider the costs and benefits. Not every program requires an extensive long-term evaluation. A program may be one that you have done for a long time and it may get good feedback. Given your resources, it may not be worth a comprehensive evaluation. Programs that get extensive evaluations are usually strategic in nature and have the attention of senior management. Training managers often conduct evaluations of these programs when they are first launched to determine whether they add value once the participants return to the job.

You may be concerned about the cost of evaluation. However, there are instances in which the data that would help evaluate your program is already collected by the organization. An example can be found in a large government agency that announced a new strategic direction. A training initiative supported the strategy. This agency had an annual employee survey that included questions such as:

- Do you understand the direction of the organization?

- Is your work directly connected to the goals of the organization?

This survey helped evaluate the training at little additional cost to the organization.

Discuss the various possibilities you have for evaluation with your consultants if they are knowledgeable in this area. The worksheet in Exhibit 14.2, Plan for Training Evaluation, is a tool to use with your consulting partners.

Exhibit 14.2. Plan for Training Evaluation.

Instructions: You and your consulting partners can use this tool as a starting point to plan your training evaluation. The evaluation plan should be finalized in the early stages of the project, because it may impact the design and follow-up activities associated with the training program.

Project: _____

Questions to Consider	Notes
What is the value of doing this evaluation?	
What is the purpose of the evaluation? • Measure program effectiveness • Determine revisions • Understand how trainees have applied what they learned • Understand impact on business • Understand factors in work environment that have helped or hindered learning and application • To influence management and get greater support in the future	
What kind of data will be needed? • Participant perceptions • Observations of supervisors • Organization/business results (sales, customer service data, costs, productivity measures, profit improvement, turnover, morale)	
What approaches should be used? (surveys, interviews, observations, analysis of available data)	
Given its importance, how comprehensive should this evaluation be? What is the associated cost?	
Who should conduct the evaluation? • Do I have the expertise? Time? Budget? • What level of objectivity is needed?	
How should roles be assigned? • Who will design the plan? • Who will conduct the evaluation? • Who will analyze the data? • Who will write the report? • Who will present the findings?	

Roles and Responsibilities in Evaluation

As you look at your evaluation plan, decide how to best use your resources. As in previous phases of your project, consider expertise, timing, cost, and context. In evaluation projects, the objectivity of a third party is often valued. The Strategic Sourcing Decision Model (Figure 3.1) found in Chapter 3 will help you. Tradeoffs are discussed below. You may outsource the evaluation completely, do it yourself, or collaborate with consultants. If engaging consultants, depending on expertise, they may or may not be the same consultants who have designed and implemented your program.

If you have funding available, you may ask consultants to do the entire project. If the evaluation involves interviews, your participants and their management may be more open with external consultants. The opposite is also true. There are certainly cultures in which employees are more likely to be open with internal resources.

Sometimes you have the time and budget, but you do not have the expertise. It is then possible to contract with consultants for coaching on how to evaluate the program. Basically, you do the evaluation, but obtain support and direction behind the scenes from the consultant. The evaluation can be a learning opportunity. In the process, you can build skills that enable you to do future evaluations independently.

If you conduct the evaluation yourself, you will need the time, budget, and expertise. Doing the evaluation on your own can be rewarding, especially if results are positive. You have the opportunity to connect with your clients again, if interviews are part of the plan. These interviews give you first-hand knowledge of how participants are using what they learned on the job. This approach also helps you stay closer to the day-to-day functioning of your organization, which may give you clues about future training that is needed. If you do the evaluation independently and consultants were previously involved, share the results with them. Everyone likes to know what impact they have had and to learn more from the experience.

If you decide to collaborate, you can assign aspects of the evaluation based on the expertise of each partner. Address the following questions:

- Who will design the evaluation plan?
- Who will implement the evaluation?

- Who will analyze the data?

- Who will write the report?

- Who will present findings to management?

When you collaborate, everyone involved gets first-hand experience learning about the program's impact. You also probably reduce the cost because you do some of the work. Evaluations can be very detailed. If you outsource the more tactical aspects, you will be free for more strategic work. Once you have the evaluation report in hand, you can communicate results to management either alone or with consultant support.

Carefully consider who should present the findings to management. Take into account the results of the evaluation study, whether or not the consultants can add value, and how management will feel about their presence. In some instances, you may want to position yourself with management as the expert and will, therefore, want to present findings on your own. If so, be sure you feel comfortable with every aspect of the evaluation and that you are able to respond to questions. In other instances, you might want to have the consultants participate as your partners. They can respond to questions and potentially help you position future initiatives or compare your results to those of other organizations. If the data is controversial, an outside perspective might be helpful. In all cases, keep in mind that, as training manager, you are the organizational leader in performance improvement efforts.

Vice President, Training and Organization Development, Fortune 100 Company

"I engaged a consulting firm to conduct a study of our training function. Each of our business units had its own training department. For many years we had tried to improve the quality of training by working with these training departments to develop common programs. However, there was redundancy and inconsistency in execution. We thought a shared services model might lead to greater efficiency and free up resources to support a greater investment in technology.

"The consultants conducted interviews throughout the organization and worked through an advisory board. The study demonstrated that reorganization would be beneficial. However, senior management was reluctant to make the needed change.

"Because the topic was controversial, I was not comfortable making the case independently. I invited the lead consultant to the meeting when we presented our findings. He was able to help senior management understand the need for the restructure and the risks associated with not making the change. He shared his experience working with other companies that had faced similar dilemmas. I never could have had the same degree of influence and appreciated his partnership."

Lesson: An external consultant can sometimes recommend solutions to management that an internal training manager could not do as effectively.

Partnership Update

After completing the evaluation, conduct another partnership update. Exhibit 14.3, the Partnership Update: Evaluation, can help you plan and conduct this conversation. Begin your conversation with the Partnership Scorecard (Exhibit 9.4) if you are using this tool. If not, conduct a more informal dialogue.

The following questions can guide your conversation:

- How effective was our evaluation?

- What did we learn?

- How well did we work together?

- What could we have done to improve our process?

- What will we do differently in the future?

This chapter has focused on evaluation of a particular initiative. The next chapter on the project wrap-up deals with evaluation as well. In this phase, you are not evaluating the training program or initiative, but the overall project and the effectiveness of the partnership with the external provider. The goal is to determine what can be learned for the future.

Exhibit 14.3. Partnership Update: Evaluation.

Instructions: Use this worksheet to help you plan the partnership update that follows the evaluation phase of your project. It provides questions you may want to explore with your consulting partners. This worksheet can be used in association with the Service Partnership Scorecard (Exhibit 9.4). Use the notes column on the right to prepare for the discussion. Document suggestions for improvement or agreements at the bottom of the page and bring these notes to future partnership updates.

Project: _____

Questions for Discussion	Notes
How would you rate the effectiveness of our evaluation? • What results did we achieve? • What did we learn about the program? • What did we learn about evaluation work that could be applied to future evaluations?	
How would you rate the effectiveness of our partnership? • If using the Service Partnership Scorecard, share ratings and comments. • If using an informal approach, rate each other against criteria for a successful partnership established at kick-off meeting.	
What could we have done to work together more effectively?	
How well have we addressed issues that we identified at previous partnership updates? • What improvements have we made? • What opportunities do we still have for the future?	
Agreements:	

■ ■ ■ ■

Key Ideas

- As outsourcing increases, the need to evaluate training becomes more important. Training should be run like a business, and measurement can help to ensure value and return on investment.

- The follow-up necessary for evaluation not only helps an organization understand the impact of training, but also helps increase results over time.

- Donald Kirkpatrick outlined four levels of training evaluation: reaction, learning, behavior, and results. Level five, return on investment, is described by Phillips and Stone.

- It is important to plan the evaluation during the early stages of the project.

- The consultant you engage to help you design and deliver a program may not have expertise or interest in designing an evaluation. You may engage another consultant to help you with this work, or you may choose to do the evaluation yourself.

- As you determine who should present the findings of an evaluation study to management, always remember that, as training manager, you are the organizational leader in performance improvement efforts.

- Conduct a partnership update after completion of the evaluation.

15

Project Wrap-Up

In the United States, there is a tendency to rush from one thing to the next. Our personal lives are as hectic as our professional lives. A typical American may run out the door in the morning, drop the kids off at school, rush to work hoping not to be late, race from meeting to meeting during the work day, and make it home for a quick dinner before it is time for a community meeting. At work no sooner do we finish one project then the next one begins. Most of us handle multiple projects, causing us to hardly notice their beginnings and endings. One project blends into another. We rarely take time to learn from projects and celebrate their completion.

Project endings bring all sorts of feelings to the surface. There is often a feeling of being let down. There may be sadness because it is the end of stimulating work and it is time to say good-bye, at least temporarily, to your consulting partners. There may be relief if the project was overwhelming or stressful. There may be satisfaction if you have accomplished your objectives. There may be feelings of appreciation between you and your consultant because of the ways in which you supported each other.

The end of a project is a time for reflection. It is an opportunity to get off the treadmill, deal with the feelings that surface, enhance learning, and celebrate both the accomplishments and the partnerships. In many cases, managers do not require you to focus on this aspect of the work. They may be just as happy if you quickly move to the next initiative. Therefore, it is up to you to stop action, pull the team together, and do the important work of the project wrap-up.

Learning Is the Goal

The project wrap-up phase is about learning from the experience. As a training manager, you work hard to improve organizational results by providing developmental experiences to strengthen the skills and knowledge of the employees in your organization. At the same time you are responsible for developing your team and yourself. Working with external partners provides an excellent opportunity for you to enhance the performance of your organization, your team, and yourself. Training managers often point to work with consultants as some of the greatest professional development experiences of their careers. By taking the opportunity to reflect on what you have learned, you will increase your likelihood of enhancing performance in the future.

In the project wrap-up phase, your goal is to look back to learn for the future. The questions that follow will help you surface the major lessons from your consulting partnerships.

- How well did the project meet its stated goals?
- How could the project have been more successful?
- How effective was the team?
- How could the team have worked more effectively?
- What are the most important lessons for the future?

The Partnership Update

The partnership update, the main focus of the project wrap-up phase, was first introduced in Chapter 9. It is a discussion in which team members assess the state of the project and the partnership and determine what improvements can be made. The partnership update should close out every critical phase of the project.

The partnership update that you conduct at this point will probably be more comprehensive than those you have conducted previously, because you are reviewing the entire project. You are also approaching the partnership update from a different vantage point. You have a longer view now and know how things turned out. You are at the end looking backward. You may be able to point to things that took place earlier in the project that might have had impact on the final results.

Exhibit 15.1, the Partnership Update: Project Wrap-Up, is a tool to help you plan and conduct the final partnership update for the project.

Exhibit 15.1. Partnership Update: Project Wrap-Up.

Instructions: Use this worksheet to help plan the final partnership update as part of the wrap-up of your project. The worksheet provides an agenda and questions you may want to explore with your consulting partners. This worksheet can be used in association with the Service Partnership Scorecard (Exhibit 9.4). Use the notes column on the right to prepare for the discussion. Document lessons learned for future projects at the bottom of the page.

Project: _____

Agenda/Questions	Notes
Welcome and objectives for meeting • To evaluate project effectiveness • To evaluate team effectiveness • To identify lessons for the future	
Project review • What results were achieved? Quantitative Qualitative • Did project achieve objectives? • What contributed to success? • What inhibited success? • How could greater results have been achieved? • What were the disappointments? • How can issues still be addressed?	
Project plan review • Reviewing each phase of the project, what went well? • What were opportunities for improvement?	
Budget review • Did team achieve the budget plan? • What were the causes of any variances to the plan? • What lessons are there for budgeting in the future? • How could the team gain greater efficiencies in the future or operate more cost-effectively?	

Exhibit 15.1. Partnership Update: Project Wrap-Up *(continued)*

Agenda/Questions	Notes
Partnership/team effectiveness • Review Partnership Scorecard or refer back to established criteria for a successful partnership • Review the following: Project planning Project management Communications Managing conflict Flexibility Quality • How well did the team work together? • What were team strengths? • What were team weaknesses? • If you worked on a similar project in the future, how could the team operate more effectively and efficiently?	
Self-development (Ask team members to consider issues of self-development prior to the meeting.) • What did team members learn from the project? • What did team members learn about themselves? • What would team members like to do to improve performance in the future?	
Celebration • Conduct a team celebration if appropriate • Have team members provide feedback/appreciation to others on the team	
Lessons for the future:	

Prepare for the Final Partnership Update

As you prepare for the final partnership update, remember that this is your last opportunity for collaboration on this particular project. Infuse your meeting with a spirit of collaboration. Schedule the final partnership update with your consulting partners and your team. Select a location that will allow you to have a meaningful dialogue. Allocate sufficient time. The amount of time will depend on the complexity of the project. You may also want to include a celebration.

Collect materials for the meeting and make copies for all participants. You may want to distribute the following documents in advance of the meeting:

- An agenda for the meeting
- The project plan
- The budget
- Program evaluation data/reports
- Final reports to management
- Notes from previous partnership updates
- Previous Partnership Scorecards

Outline objectives for the meeting and plan your agenda. Your objectives might look something like this:

- To evaluate the effectiveness of the project
- To evaluate the effectiveness of the partnership
- To identify lessons for the future

A typical agenda for the final partnership update might include the following topics:

- Welcome and review of partnership update objectives
- Project review
  - Program results
  - Project plan review
  - Budget review

- Partnership/team effectiveness review
  - Partnership scorecard review
  - What worked?
  - What could be improved for future projects?
- Lessons
  - What did individuals learn from the project?
  - What did individuals learn from working with the others on the team?
  - What did individuals learn about themselves?
- Team celebration

Conduct the Meeting

Welcome members of the team and explain the purpose of the meeting. Since you have probably had meetings with similar objectives in the past, you can relate back to these to talk about the value of getting together to evaluate the effectiveness of the work and the partnership. Point to improvements you made along the way as a result of having these kinds of meetings. Encourage openness and honesty in the dialogue.

As you step through the agenda focusing on project results, the project plan, the budget, and the partnership, use the following questions to guide your discussion:

- What did we achieve?
- What was successful?
- What could be improved for similar projects and partnerships in the future?

Assign a note-taker so you can document the lessons learned and produce a final project report. You or others can reference this report in the future if a similar project is done or the same consultants are engaged.

Your role in the meeting is to guide the discussion. Encourage all members of the team to participate. As contributions to the discussion are made, probe for more details and summarize important points to make sure everyone understands the issues. Do not rehash problems from the past unless there is more to be learned. Discuss the degree to which improvements were made along the way in response to feedback. Help the team focus on lessons for the future.

Be flexible with the agenda. It is not necessary to separate the evaluation of the work from the evaluation of the partnership. The quality of the work depends on the strength of the partnership. For example, team members may discuss how they interacted with each other when they review elements of the project plan. They might say the introduction to the workshop was not as strong as it could have been. They may acknowledge that the project team members did not take enough time to collaborate on this aspect of the training.

Results. When you discuss results, review data that is available. That data could include business results, end-of-course evaluations, or qualitative feedback. The data will depend on the nature of the project and the measures of success you identified at the outset.

Discuss how well the results met your expectations. If you were successful in achieving your objectives, what caused this success? Could the project have been more successful, more cost-effective, or time-efficient? Were there any disappointments? If so, is there an opportunity to intervene at this point to get better results? What else could be done to ensure that you sustain results over time? What role should you play? What role should your consulting partners play? What lessons have you learned regarding the achievement of results for the future? What were the key ingredients to your success that might apply to future projects? What seemed to inhibit your success and should be avoided in the future?

Project Plan Review. Step through the project plan looking at the major phases of the project. For each phase, what went well and what could have been improved? Every project is different, so it is difficult to predict what might be said for your particular project. In project reviews, team members have made the following comments:

- We probably took too long researching the topic [strategic planning] in the beginning of our work together. This meant that we were rushing in the end to put materials together, and we did not have adequate time to prepare our facilitators. Fortunately, the content was well-received. Now we can take time to enhance the materials and improve presentation skills.

- We needed to involve IT sooner. We lost time because we did not fully understand some of the system constraints.

- The simulation we developed was too basic. Although participants liked working together and had fun, the debriefing seemed superficial. What can we do to achieve a higher level of sophistication?

- The administrative support that you provided for materials was excellent. The materials looked professional and were received well in advance of the start date of the program. Participants commented on the usefulness of the job aids.

Budget Review. Jointly review the budget if appropriate. Did you meet your budget plan? Were you over or under the plan? What aspects of the project caused variances to the original plan, and why did this happen? What lessons are there for the future regarding planning and budgeting? If you plan to repeat similar initiatives, are there ways to gain greater efficiencies and operate more cost-effectively?

Partnership/Team Effectiveness Review. The degree of formality you use to evaluate the partnership will depend on your culture and on the type of project. If you are involved in a very large outsourcing project, you may tend to be more formal. If this is the case, you may want to use the Partnership Scorecard described in Chapter 9. If you plan to use this tool at the end of the project, it is probably best to use it throughout the entire project each time you conduct a partnership update. Introduce it at your kick-off meeting.

Prior to this final partnership update, complete the Partnership Scorecard and ask your consultants to do the same. The tool is helpful, but the discussion that takes place between you and your partners is more important. As you complete the scorecard, highlight strengths and weaknesses. Be as specific as possible, giving concrete examples.

If you feel an informal approach is more appropriate, the Partnership Scorecard is not necessary. Consider important aspects of the partnership. How did you work together? What worked, and what could be improved if you worked together in the future? Consider some of the following:

- Planning effectiveness

- Project management

- Meeting deadlines

- Communicating regularly

- Confronting difficult issues

- Customer service and responsiveness

- Flexibility

- Quality

Consider how you and your team performed on these aspects of the project. Consider how the consultants performed. Give each other feedback, providing specific examples.

Expanding Personal Capability

Encourage team members to look at their individual development. What did they learn from the project and the interaction with team members? What did they learn about themselves? Some teams structure this discussion by asking each team member to publicly highlight the following:

- A description of his or her most significant lesson from the project

- One area in which each would personally like to improve

- One thing he or she particularly appreciates about another member of the team

This type of conversation is an opportunity to develop greater self-awareness and provide feedback and appreciation to team members. This expression of appreciation helps bring closure to the project and provides a platform to say good-bye to others. If you plan to have this type of discussion, be sure to gain agreement from other team members in advance of the meeting. You would not want to surprise them, nor make them feel uncomfortable.

Celebration

Senior Training Executive, Energy Firm

"We conducted three major conferences for the top 450 executives of our company. Preparation for the conferences took six months. The work was challenging and stressful. The conferences were a success and our CEO was pleased. On the last day of the third conference, the project team was sitting in the meeting room that had been reserved for us. The conference was over. Team members were leaning back in their chairs exhausted with their feet up laughing about some of the funny things that had happened. We were pleased with the success of the conferences, and there was real warmth among us.

"The door opened and a waiter wheeled in a cart full of champagne and strawberries dipped in chocolate. Time to celebrate!"

Lesson: Do not miss an opportunity to celebrate your partnership. It is an important part of project closure.

Do not wait until the end of a project to celebrate and give positive feedback. Hopefully, you have found opportunities along the way to express your appreciation informally to members of the team for the unique contributions they have made. One training manager shipped her city's finest ice cream on dry ice midpoint in the development of a computerized simulation. She wanted to acknowledge the difficulty of the project and say thank you to the team.

The end of a project provides a wonderful opportunity to celebrate the results and the partnership. How you do this will depend on your culture and on the relationships you have established with your partners. A big celebration is certainly not required, and you may not feel like joyfully celebrating every project. It is inappropriate to celebrate a project that does not go well. Be authentic in the way you decide to bring your project to a close. Regardless of the outcome, it is important to understand what happened and why and to acknowledge the contributions of team members.

Celebration Ideas

There are many ways to recognize and celebrate. Exhibit 15.2, Celebrating the Partnership, provides a checklist of ideas.

What is left at this point? It is time to say "good-bye" to your partners. Hopefully, the partnership has been so positive that your final words are not "good-bye" but "until we meet again."

Your Learning Journal

Part 3, Navigating Projects While Strengthening Partnerships, ends here. Before proceeding to Part 4, Addressing the Challenges of Partnerships, take time to reflect on what you have learned and how you can build your outsourcing capability. The next page of your personal learning journal is provided (Exhibit 15.3).

Exhibit 15.2. Celebrating the Partnership.

Instructions: Look for opportunities to express appreciation and celebrate your consulting partnerships. The list below offers some suggestions for recognition and celebration.

Ideas for Appreciation and Celebration

❑ Provide feedback in the moment to your consulting partners when they do something helpful.

❑ Send a thank-you letter to your consulting partners and send a copy to their supervisor.

❑ Publicly express appreciation for consultants' contributions.

❑ Share a relaxing meal together.

❑ Send a token gift of thanks from your team.

❑ Send a token gift of thanks to employees from the consulting firm who worked behind the scenes.

❑ Send a bottle of wine or fruit basket with a note of thanks if at an off-site meeting.

❑ Send a holiday gift or card.

❑ Act as a reference for future business.

❑ Refer additional business to your consulting partners.

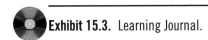

Exhibit 15.3. Learning Journal.

Navigating Projects While Strengthening Partnerships

How Can You Improve Your Outsourcing Capabilities?

Instructions: Use this learning journal to help you determine your capabilities regarding navigating projects while strengthening partnerships. Reflect on what you have learned in Part 3. For each of the aspects of a project listed below, consider what you have done in the past that has worked well. Then consider what improvements you could make for the future that would contribute to a project's success.

Aspect of Project	What Has Worked Well?	How Could You Improve Performance?
Positioning of consultants in the organization		
Your positioning in the organization		
Kick-off meetings		
Project management		
Assessment of need		

Exhibit 15.3. Learning Journal *(continued)*

Aspect of Project	What Has Worked Well?	How Could You Improve Performance?
Design and development		
Implementation		
Evaluation		
Project wrap-up		
Partnership throughout the project		

■ ■ ■ ■

Key Ideas

- The end of a project is a time for reflection, to pull the team together to do the project wrap-up.

- In the project wrap-up, you are evaluating the success of the project and the effectiveness of the partnership. The emphasis should be placed on what can be learned for the future.

- A more comprehensive partnership update should be conducted at the end of the project. Bring the following information to review:

  - Project plans

  - The budget

  - Program evaluations

  - Notes from previous partnership updates

- The final partnership update should include a review of:

  - Results

  - The project plan

  - The budget

  - The partnership and effectiveness of the team

- For all aspects of the project, you are trying to understand:

  - What was achieved?

  - What was successful?

  - What could be improved for the future?

- The wrap-up phase is a time for self-reflection, for individuals on the team to note what they have learned and how they have benefited from the project and the partnership.

- Use the final partnership update to celebrate the results you have achieved and the partnership.

Part 4

Addressing the Challenges of Partnerships

OUTSOURCED PROJECTS can present special challenges to the training manager. Part 4 addresses some of these challenges. It provides strategies for how to minimize conflict with consultants and vendors and ways to deal effectively with the conflicts that may surface on a project. The chapter on inheriting a consultant helps training managers who are new to a department evaluate projects and consulting partnerships and address issues associated with inheriting consultants and vendors. Competitive issues frequently surface when working with multiple consultants. Through Chapter 18, training managers explore ways to select consultants when more than one is involved and learn how to minimize the associated competition. Finally, consultants are often invited to do additional work in an organization beyond the training department. The last chapter of this part helps training managers explore ways they can play a role in helping to make these engagements successful.

16

Managing Conflict

Chief Learning Officer, Fortune 100 Company

"I attended a conference and heard a great speaker. I decided to hire him for a presentation to senior management. His content was strong, but I wanted him to customize his presentation and make it more interactive. We had several conversations to prepare him. He asked good questions and indicated he would customize the presentation. I was very disappointed. He didn't customize the presentation, and it wasn't interactive. I was frustrated and ended up confronting him too harshly after the program.

"Since then, I've had more experience with keynote speakers. I regret my response and wish I had waited until I felt less emotional. I also realize that most nationally recognized speakers have a prepared presentation they do time after time. It's rare for them to customize their presentations significantly.

"I wanted to use this keynote speaker the following year. This time I took a different approach. I had a conversation with him about how we could make the presentation more interactive. We decided to collaborate. He would divide his presentation into shorter segments, and I would intersperse interactive exercises. We built on our strengths."

Lesson: Be realistic about your expectations of others. When confronting difficult situations, do so at a time when you are able to contain emotions. Finally, seek collaborative and creative solutions to conflicts.

Value of Conflict

"Clashes between parties are the crucibles in which creative solutions are developed and wise tradeoffs among competing objectives are made" (Weiss & Hughes, 2005, p. 93). Even in the best partnerships, conflict occurs. Conflict is a natural part of working relationships. It is unlikely that you and another person will agree about everything. If you did, the project and the work together would be dull. Because conflict can be uncomfortable, many people shy away from it. However, effective conflict resolution can enhance a relationship between a consultant and a training manager and lead to more creative solutions.

Major philosophical differences will certainly interfere with a partnership. Hopefully, you will discover these before you hire a consultant. There are times when differences can be beneficial. For example, the person who is more global may help the project team see the big picture and the impacts of the project on the organization. The more detail-oriented person may ensure that all the logistical aspects of the program are carefully addressed. The person who comes to closure quickly may help keep the project moving along so deadlines are met. The person who needs to keep options open longer may discover a better solution.

In your consulting partnerships you will discover many differences in work styles and approaches. These can cause conflict. However, if differences can be tolerated, they can benefit the project.

In this chapter, you will find examples of typical conflicts that may occur between you and your consulting partners. Following these examples are tips that may help you minimize the possibility of conflict arising on your projects and some ways to deal effectively with the conflicts that are unavoidable.

Causes of Conflict

If conflict is natural, what are some of its causes when consultants and training managers work together? The following section describes some typical causes of conflict.

Conflict Regarding Roles and Responsibilities

Executive Coach, Independent Consultant

"A training manager of a large consumer products firm hired me to coach several managers in his company. I thought it would be a good idea for the training manager to test out the instruments we would be using. He decided to have all members of his team go through the coaching process to help the staff understand what the managers would experience.

"Over time the training manager was pleased with my work, and the managers who received the coaching were particularly complimentary. At the same time, the training manager was having difficulty dealing with a member of his staff. The employee was not meeting expectations. The training manager asked me about the feedback this staff member had received on the assessment tools. He also asked me to address the performance issues. I refused to share the feedback and was unwilling to address the performance issues. I felt the feedback was confidential. Addressing the performance issue was not in our contract, nor was it how I viewed my role. I thought it was the responsibility of the training manager to deal with the performance issues on his staff."

Lesson: Be careful to work within the boundaries of the contract and the roles you have negotiated with your consulting partners.

There are instances in which a contract calls for a consultant to help determine whether or not an employee should be retained. If that had been the case in the above example, it would have been appropriate for the consultant to address the performance issue. The training manager was fortunate that the coach was clear about the boundaries of their relationship. The coach was careful to avoid any attempt to fix things that were not his responsibility. Had the coach revealed confidential information and addressed the performance problem, there would have been a breach of trust. It easily could have caused others in the organization to have difficulty trusting the assessment/coaching process and to be wary about working in an open and honest way with the training department in the future.

It may be tempting to ask your consultant to handle difficult situations that you might want to avoid. However, it is truly not in your best interests to do this.

Lack of clarity regarding roles and responsibilities may cause conflict. There may be duplication of effort, or some tasks might not be accomplished because no one feels accountable. Team members may not be clear about where their responsibilities end and others begin. For every aspect of a project, it is important to know who is responsible and what the expectations are. Even when roles are carefully defined, conflict can surface if partners step beyond their roles or do not live up to their responsibilities. Reference original agreements when role conflict surfaces and renegotiate if necessary.

Conflict Regarding How to Work Together

Independent Consultant

"I had an overly demanding client. This client would call and expect immediate access to me. When I was available, I would take the call. But there were times when I couldn't, especially when I was with another client. The client would demand that my administrative assistant interrupt me. The first few times, I took the calls, thinking there was an emergency. However, ultimately I had to address the issue with the client. It was not acceptable for the client to interrupt me when I was working with another client."

Lesson: In all likelihood, your consultant wants to be a responsive partner and give you the best service possible. Your consultant probably has other clients. Clarify the best timing, frequency of contact, and ways to interact with your consulting partners.

A potential for conflict is the area of process—how people work together. Disagreements can arise when team members do not clarify frequency of contact. One individual believes they should meet weekly while another believes that this is too frequent. Another potential for conflict is the area of decision making. How will decisions be made? Who needs to be involved? Who has final say? What will happen if there are disagreements? Deadlines can also be a source of conflict. There can be disagreement about what it will take to develop a certain portion of a program. The training manager may need to have it sooner than the consultant feels able to produce it.

Conflict Regarding Communications

Independent Consultant, Change Management Expert

"I felt taken advantage of by the training manager. I ran several sessions on managing organizational change. The request had come from the training manager's supervisor. Although I was an expert on this topic, the sessions did not go well. I could see that the participants did not fully grasp the need for the program.

"It seemed to me that senior management had not made it clear to participants that the program was important, and the program was not tied to the business objectives of the company. I discussed my feelings with the training manager, and the training manager agreed. The training manager asked me to discuss the problem with his boss. I was naïve, but went ahead and met with the boss. The training manager's boss was furious, and I was asked to leave the project. Although I lost the contract, I learned an important lesson. It was not my responsibility to confront the issue. The problem was between the training manager and his boss.

The training manager should have communicated directly with his manager. I also realize that I should have ensured that there was good sponsorship in the beginning of the project."

Lesson: Clear and direct communications are necessary ingredients for successful partnerships.

Indirect communication, poor communication, or no communication at all can be major stumbling blocks. A consultant may think he fully understands the expectations of a project. He goes off and does significant work without checking in and getting feedback from the training manager. Because there is not regular communication, the project gets derailed and time and money are wasted.

Training managers may not clearly communicate their expectations, so members of the team do not know how to proceed. Training managers may communicate in ways that discourage dialogue. Team members are reluctant to raise important issues that need to be surfaced. There may be disagreements that never are discussed. Ultimately, communication breakdowns impact project quality.

Conflict When Friendship Is at Stake

Full partnerships with consultants can be very interesting. You spend significant time together and learn from each other. It is not unusual for friendships to evolve out of these relationships. The more you work together, the more you get to know about each other—your families, your interests, your likes, your dislikes.

Be careful about developing close friendships with consultants. They are business partners, and close personal relationships can get in the way of your ability to manage projects effectively. If you have a close friendship with a consultant you hire, you may tend to avoid conflict in order to maintain the friendship. If you decide to confront a conflict with a consultant who is your friend, you may destroy a friendship that is important to you.

Where is the boundary? You want to have positive relationships with your consultants, and it is natural to want to share personal information. As a matter of fact, it is helpful to get to know each other better as a means of building trust. It is always good to monitor how the relationship feels over time. Ask yourself the question, "If I had to confront this person regarding a difficult situation, would I still be able to do it?" If you can answer "yes" to this question, then you are probably maintaining the proper boundaries. If you cannot answer "yes" to this question, then it is probably best to step back from the friendship and maintain a more businesslike relationship.

Be careful about accepting gifts from consultants, making sure you follow your organization's guidelines. It is usually OK to accept nominal gifts. Accepting a more elaborate gift may put you in a compromised position in which you feel uncomfortable confronting a difficult situation or you feel obligated to give certain consultants business because you have accepted their gifts.

Ways to Minimize Conflict in Your Partnerships

Given the fact that conflict is a part of almost every project, what can you do to minimize it? The tips that follow may be helpful.

Discuss How You Will Deal with Conflict

At the beginning of the project, acknowledge to your consulting partners and other members of the team that conflict, or disagreement, is a natural part of the process. Let people know that you would like them to surface any issues or concerns they may have along the way and that, by doing so, they will actually enhance the working relationships and ultimate results you achieve. Then engage the team in a conversation about how they will deal with conflicts that surface. You can contribute some of the tips that follow to your discussion on how to deal with conflict.

Clarify Roles, Responsibilities, and Expectations Early

At the kick-off meeting or in the very early stages of the project, be sure to clarify expectations. If you have certain givens on the project, be sure everyone understands what these are. Are there certain components of the program that must be included? Have deadlines already been established? What do you expect in terms of quality? How do you plan to work together? What will be the frequency and type of communication? What are team member roles and responsibilities? How does each person contribute?

In the role of training manager, you do not need to know all the answers to these questions. They are topics that need to be explored with your consulting partners and team members. In the spirit of collaboration it is best if you can negotiate as much as possible.

It is important to recognize that the more clarity there is in the partnership, the better the working relationship. When roles, responsibilities, and expectations are clear, people feel more comfortable and less conflict arises. Boundaries regarding roles and responsibilities do not have to be rigid. There can and should be flexibility. Roles and responsibilities can be renegotiated if necessary. Partners sometimes run into difficulties and need support from other team members. When these kinds of needs surface, they should be discussed with the team.

Independent Consultant, Process Improvement Expert

"I was working on a process improvement initiative with other consultants. The project leader wanted all of us to use a consensus approach to decision making. It was difficult. There was disagreement about the definition of consensus and how it would be carried out. Eventually, we were asked to decide in advance the decision-making method we would use if we could not reach consensus. Everyone was surprised with the outcome. Once we had agreed on a back-up plan for decision making, we never had to use it."

Lesson: Openly discussing ways to work more effectively together will help you avoid conflict situations.

Get to Know Each Other

Work as hard on the relationship as you do on the project. Get to know your consulting partners. What are their strengths? What are their weaknesses? How do they like to work? What can they do for you? What will they need from you? Share similar information with them about yourself. This enables everyone to have realistic expectations of each other and can help avoid disappointment. It also helps you determine how you can best support each other. Getting to know each other will build trust, which is valuable to the ongoing relationship, especially when you are faced with conflict.

Provide a Regular Forum to Address Conflict

Build in time to address conflict that surfaces through the partnership update. This process is described in greater detail in Chapter 9. It is a time set aside at the end of each phase of the project to evaluate progress and the effectiveness of the partnership. This regularly scheduled update is a safety net that will help you minimize and address conflict.

Address Conflict That Arises

You can minimize the likelihood that conflict will occur. However, even with the best of intentions, you can expect some conflict on a project team. It is unavoidable. This section provides tips that can help you deal effectively with conflict situations. Each of them places priority on building and maintaining the partnership as you resolve your differences.

Surface Conflict Quickly

There is a tendency to avoid conflict. Dealing with conflict is not comfortable. However, not dealing with it can be detrimental to your project. Even if you choose to avoid dealing with a conflict, it will still exist under the surface and may have negative impact on your results. Do not allow situations to fester. Address conflict situations quickly, allowing the time necessary to resolve them appropriately. Avoid the quick fix and find long-term solutions. Many conflicts cannot be resolved in one meeting. Creative solutions often surface after people have time to reflect on the issues and possibilities. Your regular project updates and the partnership update provide good opportunities to surface and resolve conflict. However, do not wait for these if an issue has to be addressed right away.

Choose the Proper Time and Place

In a conflict, people can become emotional. If necessary, allow for a cooling-off period. If you feel very angry, it is probably best to wait and address the issue at a time when you feel calmer. Addressing the conflict in a moment of anger may cause you to escalate the conflict rather than resolve it productively. Just be careful not to delay too long and completely avoid the situation.

It may also be helpful to choose a neutral location for the discussion. At a minimum, create an atmosphere that is conducive to dialogue. Do not sit across the desk from your partner as you deal with a conflict situation. Encourage openness in the room setup. Pulling a few chairs together on the other side of the desk or going out for a cup of coffee can support a collaborative, problem-solving approach.

Avoid the "I Am Right and You Are Wrong" Stance

Blame is not helpful in conflict resolution. When conflict arises, there usually is not one person at fault. It is best to assume that both partners have contributed to the problem. Often the conflict results from the fact that the people involved simply have two points of view, both equally valid. In true partnerships, there needs to be a respect for the other and a willingness to accept differences. Admitting mistakes is not easy for most. However, doing so may decrease defensiveness in the conversation and encourage more openness for problem solving.

Use Conflict as an Opportunity to Learn

Every conflict situation provides you with an opportunity to learn—about yourself, about others, and about the situation. What went wrong? What was the cause of the problem? How did you contribute? How did the other person contribute? How can you avoid similar problems in the future?

If you approach the conflict with a goal of learning, then you are less likely to escalate the conflict. You will probably try to understand the situation and be more likely to either compromise or work to find mutually beneficial solutions.

Fully Explore the Situation

When both parties fully understand the conflict, they are more likely to find a satisfactory solution. At the beginning of your discussion, let your partner know that you are interested in solving the problem. Ask for help in resolving the differences. Share your perspectives fully with each other. Listen and be as open as you can. Avoid "you" statements, which often feels to the other person that you are blaming. Blame leads to defensiveness. Ask many questions and listen carefully so you grasp the point of view of the other person. Paraphrasing and summarizing what the other person says will ensure that you fully understand. Remember to explore how each of you may have contributed to the problem. If you take responsibility for your contribution and express this first, the other person may be willing to follow your lead.

Be Aware of How You Present Yourself

When resolving conflict, discussions can become emotionally charged. Your goal is to keep your emotions in check. Be careful with your tone of voice. Avoid shouting and aggressiveness. Watch your body language so that you do not appear threatening. Your goal is to help your partner feel comfortable and engage in a productive dialogue.

Seek Mutually Beneficial Solutions

Only after you have fully explored the situation can you find an appropriate solution. You may need to compromise or you may actually be able to find a solution that satisfies both you and your partner. How can you do this?

Remind everyone that staying focused on the objectives and the needs of the client group is the primary goal. Focusing on the objectives and the client will help everyone avoid personalizing the situation and may take some of the emotion out of the discussion.

You can engage others in brainstorming possible solutions. Ask questions such as, "How do you think we can resolve this in a mutually satisfactory way?" Listen to their ideas and build on them. Suggest your own ideas. Try to find solutions that work for everyone. Be willing to compromise.

If you reach an impasse, the following questions may help you gain a better understanding of what it would take to satisfy the other:

- What would it take to do this to your specifications?

- If we waved a magic wand, how would things work?

- What can I do to help resolve the problem?

If you are unable to find a solution, it might help to describe to the other person what will happen if you cannot solve the problem. Use this approach judiciously and try to say it with a neutral, non-threatening tone. This approach might make the other person feel uncomfortable enough to be willing to solve the problem. For example, you may say to a consultant who is unable to meet your deadline, "If we do not meet the March 1 deadline, management will no longer support the project." The consultant may then better understand the importance of meeting the deadline and maintaining management support for the project. This knowledge may encourage him or her to be more open to finding ways to solve the problem.

Express Appreciation

In all likelihood, you have both had to compromise to resolve the conflict. Express appreciation to your partner for being willing to engage in the discussion and to find a mutually beneficial solution to the problem.

When to Dissolve a Partnership

Not every partnership will work, and it may become necessary to dissolve a partnership. Deciding to dissolve a partnership is a difficult choice. You will know it is necessary if you find yourself in one of the following situations:

- There is no resolution to the conflict, and one or both partners feel that it will be impossible to continue to work together.

- The conflict cannot seem to be resolved, and it is preventing you from achieving your outcomes.

If you decide to dissolve a consulting partnership, review your contract and follow through on any obligations that have been established regarding terminating the agreement. Then have a discussion in which you explain your thinking, making respect for your consulting partner your highest priority.

This chapter is intentionally placed before the three chapters that follow on inheriting consultants, working with multiple consultants, and additional work for your consultants. These three circumstances are natural sources of conflict. As you read the next three chapters, consider the lessons regarding managing conflict as you prepare to deal with these special situations.

Key Ideas

- Conflict is a natural part of everyday working relationships. Effective conflict resolution can enhance a partnership and lead to more creative solutions.

- The following are some causes of conflict between consultants and training managers:

  - Disagreement regarding roles and responsibilities

  - Disagreement regarding how to work together

  - Disagreement regarding communications

  - Establishing too close a friendship

- The following suggestions are ways to minimize conflict when working with consultants:

  - Anticipate conflict and discuss how you will deal with it

  - Clarify roles and responsibilities early in the relationship

  - Get to know each other

  - Provide a regular forum to address conflict

- The following suggestions are ways to address conflict that arises:
  - Surface conflict quickly
  - Choose the proper time and place to address the conflict
  - Avoid the "I am right and you are wrong" stance
  - Use conflict as an opportunity to learn
  - Fully explore the conflict situation
  - Be aware of how you present yourself when resolving the conflict
  - Seek mutually beneficial solutions
  - Express appreciation for working to resolve the conflict
- If differences are too great, some partnerships may need to be dissolved.

17

Inheriting a Consultant

**Senior Vice President, Sales and Marketing Education,
Telecommunications Company**

"When I took over the training department, I inherited two consultants who had been conducting a selling skills program. The program had a great reputation in the field sales organization and a waiting list to attend. When I observed the class, I was disappointed to discover that the reputation of the program did not come from its quality but from the great stories the consultants told and the friendships they built with participants during evening social events. Quite frankly, I didn't respect them or their approach. I felt we needed a more rigorous program that relied on role play and practice.

"Although it was hard for me to continue to work with them, I decided not to terminate the relationship with these consultants. While exploring the legal and political issues, I discovered that some of my most important stakeholders thought the program was excellent. I was new and still building my reputation. I'm sure there were programs that could have had a greater impact, but the timing wasn't right. I decided to delay terminating the consultants until I had built more clout in the organization."

Lesson: Pick your battles carefully. There may be times when you feel the best decision is to terminate a relationship with a consultant, but it is not politically astute. Understand the history and political realities before taking action.

You may be new to your organization. As you examine existing programs to better understand your portfolio of offerings, you discover that your organization has contracted previously with external consultants. What should you do?

How you approach these projects and associated consultants should be similar to how you approach internally developed programs and the members of your team who are involved. The partnership framework should guide your interactions. The best outcome would be that both you and the consultants feel that they and their projects are making positive contributions to the business and that you will be able to work effectively in the future.

This chapter explores how to proceed when you have inherited projects that involve consultants, how to evaluate their contributions, and what to do if you believe the projects or the partnerships are not viable for the future.

Evaluating Existing Projects

Begin by evaluating existing projects. Before getting started, consider your own agenda and motives. How open are you to projects that existed before you arrived? Are you willing to support projects that are currently running if they are successful? Some training managers enter a system and feel they need to start all over. They find it difficult to support programs that they did not initiate, so they quickly eliminate programs that are in place. If you find something that is not working, be sure to address it. However, do not make assumptions. What existed before your arrival may be very appropriate for the future.

It is wise to announce that you plan to evaluate all projects and programs so that consultants and members of your organization do not feel you are focusing only on their pet projects. If the projects involve development or evaluation of programs, review the programs in their entirety. If they involve delivery of instruction, observe the consultants during training. The worksheet in Exhibit 17.1, Evaluating Existing Programs and Consultants, will help you determine the effectiveness of the program and the consultant.

After making your own evaluation, it is a good idea to seek the opinions of others. If members of your staff are managing these projects, they will be able to give you insight. Other sources of information would be past participants and their management. The following questions may guide your discussions:

- How would you rate the effectiveness of the program?
- In what way were you or your direct reports able to apply what was learned back on the job?
- In what ways could the program be strengthened?
- What impact is the program having on the organization?
- How would you rate the program's return on investment?
- How would you rate the effectiveness of the consultant?

After talking with those who have been involved, summarize what you have learned. What is working? What could be improved? Your next step will be to get the perspectives of the consultants and provide them with feedback. It will be important to have specific examples to support your findings.

Exhibit 17.1. Evaluating Existing Programs and Consultants.

Instructions: When you take on responsibility as the head of training, you may find existing programs that involve consultants. It is important to evaluate these programs and their associated consultants to determine their viability for the future. This worksheet can help you in that process.

Project: _____

Questions for Consideration	Notes
What is the business need for the program?	
How well is the program designed? • Are objectives clear? • Is the program engaging?	
How strong are the end-of-course evaluations?	
What is the cost of the program?	
What impact is the program having on individuals and on the organization? Are past participants: • Staying in the organization • Flourishing • Being promoted	
How effective is the consultant?	
How do others view the program? • How effective is the program? • How well were they able to apply what they learned? • What is the impact of the program on the organization? • How could the program be strengthened? • How effective is the consultant?	

Getting to Know the Consultants

After gathering background information, meet with the consultants to get their perspectives. Whether or not you have received positive feedback on their work, it is important to keep the meetings friendly and maintain the partnerships. Even if you decide not to work together on the current project, they may be consultants you might want to employ in the future. They may be potential customers of your organization. Your goals for these conversations include the following:

- Getting to know the consultants

- Getting their perspectives on the work they have been doing

- Providing them with feedback you have collected

- Exploring ways to strengthen what they are currently doing, if appropriate

Asking the following questions will help you get to know the consultants and their work:

- What is your background, including employment at other organizations and programs you have done previously?

- What is your point of view regarding this program?

- How would you evaluate the effectiveness of what you are doing for our organization?

- What impact is the project having on the participants? The organization?

- How could the program be strengthened?

Providing Feedback to the Consultants

The next stage of the conversation is to provide feedback to the consultants on their work, based on your observations and the conversations you have conducted with people who are involved.

If the Feedback Is Positive

If the feedback is positive, the next portion of the conversation is quite easy and enjoyable. Let the consultants know the positive feedback you have heard. Give them specific examples so that they will be clear about what is working and the impact the project is having.

If the feedback is positive but you think there is room for improvement, brainstorm potential ways to enhance the work. Remember, this is a partnership so ask the consultants for their ideas on how to improve what they are doing. Give your suggestions. Jointly determine the changes that will be made and next steps. Set target dates for enhancements and document your agreements.

Whether or not the work needs improvement, establish agreements regarding how you will work together in the future. Discuss the frequency of future contact. How will you continue to communicate with each other? Will phone contact be sufficient? Will there be face-to-face meetings? Are there future projects that need to be planned? How will you continue to measure the impact of their work? What other issues are important to address? How can you support them and help them be successful? You may need to renegotiate their reporting relationship if there have been any changes since your arrival.

New Training Manager, Banking Institution

"What a pleasant surprise. I was new in my assignment and set an appointment to meet with a consultant who had worked for the training department for years. The consultant was well-perceived. Feedback on his performance was strong, and I planned to continue his contract.

"When we met we ended up in a three-hour conversation. I discovered that he had a wealth of information about the company. He provided information about the program he facilitated. He gave me his observations about the culture and made several suggestions for areas the training department could tackle in the future. I discovered a new partner."

Lesson: Because consultants operate from a distance, they can provide important feedback about your organization and its culture. Seek out this information from your consulting partners. It can be helpful as you interact with management and plan future initiatives.

If Feedback Is Negative

If feedback is negative, you have two choices. You can either work with the consultants to improve their performance, or you can terminate the relationship. If you decide to work with them to improve, you can continue the conversation. If you think you would like to terminate the relationship, there is more work to prepare for this conversation. You should not have a discussion with the consultants about termination at this point.

Working to Improve Their Performance. If you think their performance can be improved, discuss the feedback with the consultants. There will be some positives, so let them know what is working and why and give specific examples. Do they agree or disagree? How do they see the situation? Find opportunities to demonstrate your support for them and their work. Let them know that you would like to continue your work together, but that issues need to be resolved.

The next phase of the conversation is similar to suggestions outlined above when feedback is generally positive but there is room for improvement. Ask the consultants how they think the issues should be resolved. Give your ideas. Explore the various possibilities, and then come to agreement on needed changes. Discuss how and when these changes will be implemented and agree to an action plan. Set target dates to follow up. Document your agreements so that everyone understands the changes that are needed and how they will be accomplished. Depending on the extent and complexity of the needed changes, you may want to follow up with a more extensive conversation at a later date or schedule a series of meetings to be sure issues are resolved.

Terminating the Relationship. You may be dissatisfied with the consultants' performance and decide to terminate the relationship. Move cautiously if this is the case.

There may be legal issues to consider. There also may be political ramifications to your decision.

Begin by reviewing the contract that was negotiated originally. What are the implications of terminating the relationship? Are there costs? Do you need to give them notice? If so, how much notice is required? If you are not certain of the answers to these questions, it is best to consult legal counsel.

Consider the political aspects of your decision to terminate the relationship. What relationship do the consultants have with others in your organization? Who engaged them initially? Are they still in your organization? How will they react, and will this impact you? How will your manager react to the termination? How is the initiative perceived throughout the organization? Consider whose support you need to terminate the relationship.

Once you have determined the legal requirements, have analyzed the political ramifications, and believe you have the support to terminate the consultants, you are ready to proceed. Meet with the consultants and explain your decision. Help them understand how you came to the decision and why their work is no longer needed. Their work may no longer fit with the organization's current priorities, or it may not have the impact that is needed. Since this conversation may be difficult, you may want to involve someone else in the meeting—the original sponsor or your manager. Whatever the reason for your decision, be honest, respectful, and sensitive to the feelings of the consultants.

Working with Consultants When There Is No Chemistry

The first example in this chapter raises the issue of how to deal with consultants when there is no chemistry between you. It was difficult for the manager in the telecommunications firm to continue to work with the sales training consultants because she did not respect their work. This situation could also arise if you feel you have to hire a consultant who has specific expertise, but you do not particularly feel you have rapport with that person. Partnerships work best when there is chemistry. So what can you do?

If you are caught in a situation in which you do not have rapport with consultants you need to engage, keep focused on the outcomes of the project. The greatest risk is that you will avoid contact with them or allow the lack of rapport to interfere with the quality of the initiative. Try to identify the source of the problem. If it is something that you can address, do so. Chapter 16 on managing conflict provides guidance. If it is an issue that you feel you cannot address, such as a personality clash, make sure you do what is necessary to manage the project. Set regular appointments to update with the consultants. Review the project, making sure it stays on track. Address issues as they surface. Look for the positives in the relationship and try to build on these. Although there is no guarantee, it is possible that over time you may be able to build greater rapport.

In summary, when you take on a new position and inherit consultants, building partnerships with existing consultants is a key to your success. The next chapter focuses on initiatives for which you need to work with multiple consultants. You will not only need to build partnerships with these consultants, but you will also need to help them work collaboratively with each other. Chapter 18 provides support as you work with multiple consultants.

Key Ideas

- When you take on responsibility to lead a training function, you may find that the training organization has been contracting with external consultants. It is important to evaluate the programs and the consultants and determine their future viability.

- Be careful about your motives when evaluating existing programs, whether they involve consultants or are internal programs. Do not assume that existing programs are unworkable for the future. Suspend judgment until you fully understand the programs and the consultants. They may be important programs and relationships for the future.

- Assess programs in which consultants are involved. Review the content, observe them, and gather feedback from past participants and others who are in a position to evaluate their effectiveness.

- Get to know the consultants who provide services to your department. Identify their strengths and the contributions they are making. Solicit their feedback on programs and on your organization. They can provide you with valuable information about your organization and its training needs.

- Provide feedback to consultants and determine next steps. Look for ways to strengthen programs, if appropriate.

- If you decide to terminate a relationship with a consultant, consider the legal and political ramifications.

18

Working with Multiple Consultants

Director of Training, Hospital

"I hired two consultants to facilitate a program. While observing one of the sessions, I could see the competition between them. They competed for air time on the agenda, and one of the consultants made a few humorous, unsupportive remarks about the other. I felt that their behavior had a negative impact on the program. I invited both to a meeting to discuss my observations. The meeting was uncomfortable. One consultant said she felt overshadowed by the other. He interrupted her constantly. I made it clear that collaboration was a requirement. Eventually they relaxed and were able to negotiate guidelines for team teaching."

Lesson: There may be competition between consultants. Competitive issues in partnerships must be addressed so that they do not interfere with performance.

Some projects require you to hire multiple consultants. There may not be one consultant who can meet all of your needs for a particular project. Utilizing more than one consultant brings variety, interest, and a broader perspective to your initiatives. However, getting various consultants to collaborate can be a challenge. Selecting consultants who are willing and able to collaborate is important when you find yourself in this situation. This chapter will help you determine when to hire multiple consultants and how to manage these relationships.

Why Hire Multiple Consultants

There are many circumstances in which a training manager may need multiple consultants. Some examples follow.

- You are outsourcing your entire training function. Based on curriculum needs, you have selected three major vendors. There is not one vendor who has the expertise to provide all the training. In addition, you do not want to be dependent on any one vendor. You recognize, however, that if the three vendors collaborate, your participants could benefit substantially. Each of the vendor partners potentially could reinforce the work of the others.

- You are conducting a leadership program for high-potential executives. You have contracted with a consulting firm that specializes in leadership development. In addition, the curriculum requires you to hire a faculty member from a prestigious university to serve as a keynote speaker. You are also working with a vendor who develops computer-based training. This vendor is developing a computerized simulation that will be used throughout the program. Your goal is to provide a seamless experience for participants. Integration of all pieces of the program will require the entire team to collaborate.

- As training manager, you are supporting a major culture change initiative in your organization. The change requires all employees in your company to attend a two-day conference in which the organization's new vision, values, and goals will be explored. The conference will include presentations by senior management and several break-out sessions. You have hired ten consultants to facilitate these break-out sessions. They must work together effectively so that there is consistency.

If it is necessary to hire several consultants for a project, you may be able to work with a larger consulting firm who can provide all the resources. Members of the same firm may be easier to manage, since they typically know each other and may have worked together previously. If you choose to hire consultants from a variety of sources, the sections that follow may be helpful.

Selection Considerations When There Are Multiple Consultants

Independent consultants are often just that—independent. They frequently select a career in consulting because they enjoy the freedom it offers, and they prefer the role of individual contributor. Because they have chosen to work outside an organization, their external perspective often gives them the ability to see a situation more clearly. This quality, in addition to others, is exactly the reason you want to engage them. It also might make it difficult for some consultants to collaborate.

Feelings of competition may be triggered when multiple consultants are involved on a project. Competitive feelings may be more typical of consultants who have their own practices. Consultants who work for larger firms usually have stronger needs for affiliation and are more accustomed to collaborating with colleagues. Regardless of who you hire, you will want to identify those consultants who have both the interest and ability to collaborate when multiple consultants are involved.

When selecting consultants for these projects, the selection criteria outlined in Part 2, on identifying and selecting consultants, apply. You want to be sure that the consultants you hire have the expertise, that their pricing fits within your budget, that they have the resources you require, that they have a customer orientation, and that they are a good fit for your organization and that you are comfortable with them. It is important to assess their ability to collaborate.

As in any interviewing and selection process, the past is a good predictor of the future. Finding out how perspective consultants have collaborated in the past will let you know about their ability to collaborate in the future. You can make an assessment during the interview process and when you check references. The worksheet that follows, Interviewing and Checking References When Multiple Consultants Are Involved (Exhibit 18.1), can serve as a springboard for planning your questions. When speaking with potential consultants, ask questions regarding their ability to collaborate and find out about times when they had to work with other consultants.

As the consultant responds, listen for interest and ability to collaborate. Does the consultant seem to enjoy collaboration and feel there is something to be learned in the process? Would the person like to do a similar project again in the future?

When checking references, let the former employer or project manager know that the project will require collaboration with other consultants. Some questions you might use are included in Exhibit 18.1.

Setting Expectations Regarding Collaboration

Before hiring consultants, let them know about the need to collaborate with other consultants. Explain who the other consultants are and clarify roles and responsibilities. Indicate when and how you will want the consultants to interact with each other to ensure good communication and a partnership. Confirm their interest in collaborating. Consultants not interested in collaborating may eliminate themselves.

When you hold the project kick-off meeting, it is important to reiterate your expectations for partnership. Stress to all consultants involved that you place a high value on collaboration and that working together effectively will be important to the success of the project. Clarify roles and responsibilities of all consultants who are working on the project so that they understand the relationship between their work and the work of others.

Communication will be a key to ensuring the collaboration. Discuss expectations for communication. Will there be regular meetings or conference calls? Establish these expectations early and get these meetings on the calendar so you have full participation.

Exhibit 18.1. Interviewing and Checking References When Multiple Consultants Are Involved.

Instructions: When engaging multiple consultants on a project, you will want to be sure they can collaborate. The questions on this worksheet can be used in the interviewing and reference checking stages of hiring consultants. They will help you evaluate the willingness and ability of consultants to collaborate with other consultants.

Project: _____

Consultant: _____

Questions	Notes
Interviewing the Consultant	
Tell me about a time when you worked with other consultants on a project. • What was the experience like? • How did you handle the various roles on the project? • What did you like about the experience? • What was not satisfying about working with other consultants on the project? • What conflicts surfaced? • How did you resolve conflicts? • If you had to do the project again, what would you do differently?	
How do you feel about collaboration with other consultants?	
What concerns do you have?	
Checking References	
Did the consultant have to collaborate with other consultants while working for you?	
How well were they able to collaborate? Please provide an example.	
What conflicts surfaced, and did the consultant deal with them appropriately?	
How would you rate the ability of this consultant to collaborate with other consultants? Please explain.	

Managing Projects with Multiple Consultants

Your plan for utilizing consultants, along with the roles they assume on a project, will help determine how to manage the relationships. There are different degrees of collaboration that may be required, depending on the particular project. The sections that follow provide some examples that may be similar to initiatives you manage in your organization.

Multiple Consultants and Distinct Responsibilities

If your consultants have distinct responsibilities, then the collaboration will probably be easier. There is less likelihood of overlap and competition. In this case, your primary goal is to help the various consultants understand what the other consultants will do and to look for opportunities for them to support each other, if appropriate.

Director, Training, Insurance Industry

"We were delivering a multiple-day leadership program. Early in the week an expert on industry trends delivered a presentation. A key issue was the anticipated retirement of a significant number of employees over the next ten years. This trend made it more important for the organization to develop the leadership capabilities of the next generation of leaders. The consultant who delivered the segment on coaching later in the program referenced this trend to help motivate participants to become better coaches. I was pleased because I had spent significant time in advance of the program helping each of the presenters understand the content of the other presenters. It enhanced the learning and created a more cohesive experience."

Lesson: To ensure a cohesive experience for participants, the training manager must encourage collaboration among consultants and work closely with them to find opportunities to integrate their work.

Multiple Consultants and Similarities in Responsibilities

If your consultants have similar responsibilities, then the collaboration will probably be more complex. The likelihood of competition is greater. Your primary goal is to help the various consultants understand what the other consultants will do and to help them find opportunities to support each other.

Chief Learning Officer, Insurance Industry

"We were trying to shift from a process-oriented culture to a service and selling culture. Recognizing that this was an enormous undertaking that would take years, we decided that every employee in the company needed to have a significant experience that would help launch the cultural change. As a result, every employee participated in an off-site event in which senior management addressed the group about the future of the company and the culture that would be required for success. The company used learning maps to help employees understand the competitive environment, the direction of the organization, its structure, and its source of profit in the marketplace.

"Given the size of our organization, we held over fifty meetings with approximately 250 employees attending each meeting. This approach required us to use an outside firm that hired twenty consultants to serve as facilitators. All facilitators had the same responsibilities: to interface with senior leaders, facilitate discussion using the learning maps, and provide feedback to management on the process.

"Because the organization wanted a consistent experience for all employees, I met regularly with all the consultants. All consultants participated in meetings at the beginning of the project to understand their roles and to be trained to facilitate the maps. Emphasis was placed on the importance of collaboration. At the end of each conference, all consultants were required to attend a meeting to debrief the experience. They discussed what went well, what did not, and what changes were needed for the future. This process helped consultants work effectively together and gave senior management feedback about employee reaction to the new company direction."

Lesson: It takes a significant investment of time to manage a project with multiple consultants when collaboration is required. The training manager must build in processes that encourage cooperation among consultants.

What If Competition Surfaces?

As the manager of the project, regularly check with the consultants to monitor the ongoing collaboration. As you ask for feedback, consider the following questions:

- From your perspective, how is the project going?
- What is working?
- What is not working?
- What could we do to improve our results?
- How are things going with the consultants on the team? Are you satisfied with the level of collaboration?
- What can you do differently to improve collaboration?

In these conversations, you will discover ways to improve the program. You will also be able to assess the working relationships on the team. If you sense that some consultants are not establishing positive working relationships with others, address these issues immediately. Lack of partnership will impact the quality of the work. If necessary, be prepared to mediate conflicts on the team. Remind the consultants that you expect them to be role models for collaboration for your organization.

Partnership Updates with Multiple Consultants

The partnership update is even more important when multiple consultants are involved. The greater the number of people on your project team, the greater the complexity of the project. If consultants have similar responsibilities, there is a greater likelihood of competition and conflict. The partnership update can help you address these issues among your consultants.

If you engage top-quality consultants, it is likely that other departments may want to engage them for additional work. Political issues can surface easily. Chapter 19 will help you handle situations in which consultants contract for additional work in your organization.

◼ ◼ ◼ ◼

Key Ideas

- It is not unusual for competition to surface when you engage multiple consultants on the same project.

- When hiring multiple consultants for a project, be sure they have the ability and willingness to collaborate.

- Before hiring consultants, it is important to set expectations regarding the need to collaborate with other consultants.

- The training manager needs to facilitate the collaboration between consultants, helping them see how their work is related and how they can reinforce each other's work.

- The training manager needs to put processes in place that encourage collaboration.

- Regularly update with consultants who are working on projects with other consultants. Find out what is going well and where improvements might be needed. Pay particular attention to the collaboration. Confront issues of competition that surface.

19

Additional Work for Your Consultants

Training Director, National Specialty Retailer

"I hired an e-learning firm to develop product training. The training was well-received by the sales force, especially since there was no need to travel to headquarters. Because the training was such a positive experience, a line manager from one of the divisions decided to contract with the same firm to develop financial skills training. This line manager had little experience working with consultants and no experience developing training. He never informed me about the project. When the program was complete, there were major technical difficulties, because there had been minimal contact with the IT department. The $250,000 program was never actually implemented."

Lesson: Educate your organization about the importance of involving your department when outsourcing training. Stay close to these projects. Managers usually do not have experience working with training consultants and may be unaware of how to manage these projects successfully.

It is not unusual for your internal clients to hire your consultants for additional work. In all likelihood, your internal clients have had positive interactions with the consultants, and they may have issues the consultants could help them address. You may not have the resources to support these additional projects.

Even though you may not do the work yourself, it is important to maintain contact with both the consultants and your internal clients in these situations. This chapter will discuss the role you should play when consultants contract for additional work in your organization.

Importance of Setting Expectations Regarding Additional Work

As you analyze the above example, many questions come to mind. What is the training strategy for the organization? What are the expectations for communications between a line manager and the training department? How are decisions regarding new training initiatives made? Who needs to be involved? Can a department contract for its own training, or is the training department involvement or approval required?

These are important considerations, but beyond the purview of this book. When working in partnership with consultants, clarify your expectations so that they understand how to proceed when they are invited to do additional work in your organization. It is also a good idea to let others in your organization know that you prefer to be informed when training consultants are hired. Your organization may be able to avoid problems similar to the one described above if you are kept informed.

Your Role When There Is Additional Work

As you think through your expectations for consultants when there is additional work, determine to what degree you think you need to be involved. Your involvement may vary depending on your culture. In highly decentralized organizations, it may not be necessary for you to be involved at all. In a highly centralized setting, you may need to be involved every step of the way. The degree of your involvement may also depend on the particular objectives of the project, on your expertise, and potentially on your workload.

At a minimum, consultants should let you know that they have been invited to do additional work in your organization. Letting you know is common courtesy in good partnerships. Explain to consultants that you want to be informed if they are approached by other departments. It is best to inform them early in your partnership, because they may be approached even before the completion of your project.

When consultants let you know they are contracting for new work, it gives you the opportunity to determine how, if at all, you want to be involved. It also enables you to help the consultants understand organizational issues that may be related to the work. This kind of information can help them to be more successful. The information you share will be similar to the kind of information outlined in Chapter 9 and might include things such as political issues, description of key personnel, organizational structure, etc.

It is a good idea to encourage consultants to touch base with you regularly throughout the project to keep you informed. You may be able to help them interpret issues or deal more effectively with the new people they encounter. In a sense, you may become their consultant on the new project.

It is also important for you to communicate with the key contacts in the departments who are contracting for consulting services. These individuals may not be as experienced as you in working with consultants. You may be able to provide coaching and even share a copy of this book with them to help them develop better partnerships with consultants. Even if they are experienced in working with consultants, you have more experience working with these particular consultants. You will be able to describe their strengths and weaknesses and give tips on how to work most effectively with them.

Organization Development Consultant

"I served as a facilitator for a senior leadership training program for a pharmaceuticals firm for many years. I had a good partnership with the training manager who hired me, and I had built a strong reputation. A sales division of the company contacted me to facilitate a program that focused on improving sales performance. Sales performance had reached a plateau in the last two years. I met with the senior leadership of the division and then presented a plan that included facilitating some initial meetings with the management team, followed by coaching and selling skills training.

"In an unrelated conversation with the training manager, I mentioned the work I would be doing for the sales division. The training manager suggested we get together to review the plan. She explained some changes in the organization that would result in the implementation of a new corporate sales training program. I appreciated receiving this information. I certainly didn't want to introduce a model for selling in the division that would be replaced within six months."

Lesson: When line managers outsource training projects, you can help ensure that the programs are aligned with the organization's overall training strategy.

Your Learning Journal

Part 4, Addressing the Challenges of Partnerships, ends here. Before proceeding to Part 5, Expanding Your Personal Capability, take time to reflect on what you have learned and on how you can build your outsourcing capability. Exhibit 19.1, the next page of your personal learning journal is provided here.

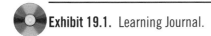**Exhibit 19.1.** Learning Journal.

Addressing the Challenges of Partnerships

How Can You Improve Your Outsourcing Capabilities?

Instructions: Use this learning journal to help you determine your capabilities regarding addressing the challenges of partnerships. Reflect on initiatives you have outsourced. Consider the questions below to help you summarize what you have learned in Part 4 and determine ways to improve your performance.

1. What have been the causes of conflicts that have surfaced on your outsourced initiatives?

2. What could you do to minimize conflict or address conflict more effectively on future projects?

3. What lessons have you learned for the future when dealing with consultants you have inherited?

4. What lessons have you learned for the future when hiring and working with multiple consultants?

5. What lessons have you learned for the future regarding situations in which your consultants have obtained additional work in your organization?

Key Ideas

- Educate your organization about the importance of involving your department when hiring consultants to outsource training.

- Let consultants know that you want to be informed if they are invited to do additional work in your organization.

- You may be able to help the consultant understand the context of the new project, including cultural issues, strategic direction, political issues, the leadership, and upcoming organizational changes.

- Since you have experience working with the consultant, you may be able to help the manager work more effectively with the consultant.

- When line managers outsource training projects, your involvement can help ensure that the programs are aligned with the organization's overall training strategy.

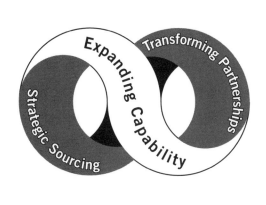

Part 5

Expanding Your Personal Capability

Chapter 20   A Development Plan

PART 5 assists training managers in summarizing what they have learned. It encourages them to review their learning journals with a focus on how to build their capability as outsourcing partners. They explore their strengths and opportunities for improvement and build development plans to improve performance.

A Development Plan

OUTSOURCING IS NOT EASY. The projects you outsource may present some of the greatest challenges of your career. If well-managed, these projects and their associated partnerships have the potential to be the most rewarding. They provide tremendous opportunities for personal and professional growth.

This chapter of the book is designed as a culminating experience. It will help you reflect on what you have learned about outsourcing, review your personal learning journal, and build a development plan to strengthen your capabilities as an outsourcing partner. Record your plan using Exhibit 20.1, Your Development Plan.

Step I: Review Your Learning Journal

Begin by gathering the completed pages of your learning journal from the end of each major part of this book. Reflect on the self-assessment that you completed at the end of Chapter 2, Guiding Principles. Now that you have a clearer understanding of outsourcing, how would you rate yourself on the various capabilities required for successful outsourcing? Would you rate yourself the same? Would you make any changes? Revise the self-assessment if you now have a different point of view on your skills.

Look at each of the remaining pages of your learning journal. Identify strengths and areas for development. Do you notice any themes as you review the journal? Are you stronger in some of the strategic aspects of outsourcing? Do your strengths seem to be more in the area of developing partnerships? Perhaps you have some strengths and weaknesses in each of these areas.

Step II: Identify Strengths and Areas for Improvement

Utilizing the final page of the learning journal, Your Development Plan, list your top three strengths in outsourcing. Now list your top three areas for improvement.

Step III: Identify Ways to Leverage Strengths

Continue using this development planning form. Consider your strengths in outsourcing. These are skills to leverage on your outsourced projects. How can you build on these strengths on current or future projects? List ways you can take better advantage of these capabilities.

For example, if you have listed the skill, "Apply change management principles to achieve outcomes of outsourced initiatives" as a strength, how could you leverage this strength on an existing project? Could you take another look at a project you are working on and determine additional ways to ensure its success from a change management standpoint? Are there additional stakeholders to influence? Could you ask management to play a stronger role in

**Exhibit 20.1.** Learning Journal.

Your Development Plan

Instructions: Use this worksheet to summarize your learning journal and build a plan for development. Review and, if necessary, revise the self-assessment that you completed at the end of Chapter 2 on guiding principles. Identify themes from the notes you took in your learning journal. List your top three strengths and top three areas for improvement. Identify ways to leverage strengths and improve performance in outsourcing.

Strengths

    1.

    2.

    3.

Areas for Improvement

    1.

    2.

    3.

Ways to Leverage Strengths

    1.

    2.

    3.

Ways to Improve Performance

    1.

    2.

    3.

following up to ensure the success of the program? Could you mentor others who are involved and help them better understand the change process?

Step IV: Identify Ways to Improve Performance

Examine areas for improvement. What themes are evident? What could you do to strengthen these skills? List your ideas for improvement on the development planning form. Did any ideas surface as you read this book that might be helpful?

For example, if there have been frequent breakdowns in communication on an existing project, can you contact your outsourcing partner and discuss the issue? Could you set regular updates for the future? Can you take better advantage of the partnership update process?

Identifying ways to improve can be difficult. Consider the following options:

- Solicit feedback from your outsourcing partners on what you can do to improve.

- Solicit feedback from other members of your team.

- Identify colleagues who seem to be successful at outsourcing. Ask them to explain how they successfully manage outsourced projects. What suggestions do they have on how best to approach the aspects of your project that you find difficult?

- Do further reading and research online about outsourcing. These websites may be helpful:

  - www.trainingoutsourcing.com

  - www.outsourcing-center.com

- Identify conferences on the topic of outsourcing training.

  - Check www.astd.org/astd/Conferences/Outsourcing.htm for the ASTD annual outsourcing conference.

  - Check www.trainingoutsourcing.com and click on "upcoming events"

- Identify additional development suggestions from the following resources:

  - *The Successful Manager's Handbook* (Gebelein, Nelson-Neuhaus, Skube, Lee, Stevens, Hellervik, & Davis, 2004)

  - *For Your Improvement* (Lombardo & Eichinger, 2003)

Step V: Measure Your Progress

After identifying specific action steps for your development plan, determine how you will measure your progress. How will you know that you are making improvements?

Sharing your development plan with a colleague, especially one who can observe you in action, is a great approach. Somehow, when you make your development plan public, you are more likely to make progress. If someone is aware of your development goals and can observe and give you feedback, you are even more likely to improve.

If you have gone to your outsourcing partners and asked the question, "What can I do to be a better outsourcing partner?" these individuals can also give you feedback. Go back to them from time to time and ask how you are doing. Be patient. Even if you change your behavior, it often takes longer for their perceptions to change. Keep practicing. Your efforts will pay off in the long run. Your outsourced projects will get easier with more experience.

Some Final Words on Your Development

You may be uncertain of yourself in outsourcing partnerships. Perhaps you have not had much experience. Perhaps you have had difficult experiences. You may know that you have some developmental opportunities and may not be sure how to proceed. Stop action. Consider what you want from your outsourcing partners. How do you want them to interact with you?

Maister, Green, and Galford, in *The Trusted Advisor,* identify a list of twenty-two traits that the average person wants from trusted advisors, people who advise them on important business, career, and perhaps even personal decisions. Some of the traits include:

- Seem to understand and like us

- Are consistent

- Don't panic or become overemotional

- Act like a real person, not someone in a role

- Tell us the truth (Maister, Green, & Galford, 2000, pp. 4–5).

Well, in reality, trusted advisors like your outsourcing partners want the same things from you as you want from them. So if you are not certain how to proceed, approach the situation from their perspective. What would your partners want from you? If you are unclear, ask what would be most helpful. With authenticity, you will build trust. With trust, you will build partnerships. With partnerships, you will build success.

Best of luck with your outsourcing partners and your outsourced initiatives!

References

Anderson, M. (2000). Outsourcing as a strategic tool to enhance learning. In J. Phillips (Ed.), *Building learning capability through outsourcing.* Alexandria, VA: American Society for Training & Development.

Anderson, M. (2003). *Bottom-line organization development: Implementing & evaluating strategic change for lasting value.* Burlington, MA: Butterworth-Heinemann.

Bell, C.R., & Shea, H. (1998). *Dance lessons: Six steps to great partnerships in business & life.* San Francisco, CA: Berrett-Koehler.

Block, P. (2000). *Flawless consulting* (2nd ed.). San Francisco, CA: Pfeiffer.

Covey, S. (1989). *The 7 habits of highly effective people.* New York: Simon & Schuster.

Davis, P., Naughton, J., & Rothwell, W. (2004). New roles and new competencies for the profession. *T&D, 59*(4), 26-36.

DeViney, N., & Sugrue, B. (2004). Learning outsourcing: A reality check. *T&D, 59*(12), 40–45.

Dolezalek, H. (2005). The 2005 industry report. *Training, 2*(12), 14–28.

Gebelein, S.H., Nelson-Neuhaus, K.J., Skube, C.J., Lee, D.G., Stevens, L.A., Hellervik, L.W., & Davis, B.L. (2004). *Successful manager's handbook.* Minneapolis, MN: Personnel Decisions International.

Hall, B. (2004). Time to outsource? *Training, 41*(6), 14.

Harris, P. (2004). Outsourced training begins to find its niche. *T&D, 59*(11), 36–42.

Harward, D. (2003). *Defining requirements for training outsourcing services.* Durham, NC: TrainingOutsourcing.com LLC.

Kirkpatrick, D.L. (1994). *Evaluating training programs: The four levels.* San Francisco, CA: Berrett-Koehler.

Lombardo, M., & Eichinger, R. (2003). *For your improvement: A development and coaching guide.* Minneapolis, MN: Lominger Limited.

Maister, D.H., Green, C.H., & Galford, R.M. (2000). *The trusted advisor.* New York: Touchstone/Simon & Schuster.

Phillips, J., & Stone, R. (2002). *How to measure training results: A practical guide to tracking the six key indicators.* New York: McGraw-Hill.

Sugrue, B., & Rivera, R. (2005). *ASTD 2005 state of the industry report.* Alexandria, VA: ASTD.

Weiss, J., & Hughes, J. (2005). Want collaboration? Accept and actively manage conflict. *Harvard Business Review, 83*(3), 93.

About the Author

Debbie Friedman is operating vice president at Federated Department Stores, where she heads Federated Leadership Institute, a training function whose mission is to strengthen the leadership capabilities of the top 1,800 executives. The focus of the Institute is to:

- Help leaders make an effective transition as they step up to broader responsibilities in the company
- Prepare high-potential executives for senior-level assignments

Partnership between Debbie, her staff, and external training and organization development providers is a key to the success of the Institute. Federated has been named for two years as one of the Top 100 Companies in Training and Development by *Training* Magazine. They have also received a Best Practice Award by the National Retail Federation for the work of the Leadership Institute.

Over her nineteen years with Federated, Debbie has managed numerous large-scale projects that have involved multiple vendors and consultants. Debbie considers managing vendor relationships one of the most challenging aspects of her job.

She has held other training positions at Federated, including director of training at Lazarus, a Midwest division, and at AT&T in the Sales and Marketing Education Organization. Debbie brings a background in university career planning and placement work and classroom teaching to her corporate training experience.

Debbie holds a master's in education from Xavier University (Cincinnati) and a bachelor of arts from Stern College for Women, Yeshiva University. She has published articles in professional journals and has spoken on numerous occasions at national, regional, and local conferences.

Index

Pfeiffer Publications Guide

This guide is designed to familiarize you with the various types of Pfeiffer publications. The formats section describes the various types of products that we publish; the methodologies section describes the many different ways that content might be provided within a product. We also provide a list of the topic areas in which we publish.

FORMATS

In addition to its extensive book-publishing program, Pfeiffer offers content in an array of formats, from fieldbooks for the practitioner to complete, ready-to-use training packages that support group learning.

FIELDBOOK Designed to provide information and guidance to practitioners in the midst of action. Most fieldbooks are companions to another, sometimes earlier, work, from which its ideas are derived; the fieldbook makes practical what was theoretical in the original text. Fieldbooks can certainly be read from cover to cover. More likely, though, you'll find yourself bouncing around following a particular theme, or dipping in as the mood, and the situation, dictate.

HANDBOOK A contributed volume of work on a single topic, comprising an eclectic mix of ideas, case studies, and best practices sourced by practitioners and experts in the field.

An editor or team of editors usually is appointed to seek out contributors and to evaluate content for relevance to the topic. Think of a handbook not as a ready-to-eat meal, but as a cookbook of ingredients that enables you to create the most fitting experience for the occasion.

RESOURCE Materials designed to support group learning. They come in many forms: a complete, ready-to-use exercise (such as a game); a comprehensive resource on one topic (such as conflict management) containing a variety of methods and approaches; or a collection of like-minded activities (such as icebreakers) on multiple subjects and situations.

TRAINING PACKAGE An entire, ready-to-use learning program that focuses on a particular topic or skill. All packages comprise a guide for the facilitator/trainer and a workbook for the participants. Some packages are supported with additional media—such as video—or learning aids, instruments, or other devices to help participants understand concepts or practice and develop skills.

- *Facilitator/trainer's guide* Contains an introduction to the program, advice on how to organize and facilitate the learning event, and step-by-step instructor notes. The guide also contains copies of presentation materials—handouts, presentations, and overhead designs, for example—used in the program.

- *Participant's workbook* Contains exercises and reading materials that support the learning goal and serves as a valuable reference and support guide for participants in the weeks and months that follow the learning event. Typically, each participant will require his or her own workbook.

ELECTRONIC CD-ROMs and web-based products transform static Pfeiffer content into dynamic, interactive experiences. Designed to take advantage of the searchability, automation, and ease-of-use that technology provides, our e-products bring convenience and immediate accessibility to your workspace.

METHODOLOGIES

CASE STUDY A presentation, in narrative form, of an actual event that has occurred inside an organization. Case studies are not prescriptive, nor are they used to prove a point; they are designed to develop critical analysis and decision-making skills. A case study has a specific time frame, specifies a sequence of events, is narrative in structure, and contains a plot structure—an issue (what should be/have been done?). Use case studies when the goal is to enable participants to apply previously learned theories to the circumstances in the case, decide what is pertinent, identify the real issues, decide what should have been done, and develop a plan of action.

ENERGIZER A short activity that develops readiness for the next session or learning event. Energizers are most commonly used after a break or lunch to stimulate or refocus the group. Many involve some form of physical activity, so they are a useful way to counter post-lunch lethargy. Other uses include transitioning from one topic to another, where "mental" distancing is important.

EXPERIENTIAL LEARNING ACTIVITY (ELA) A facilitator-led intervention that moves participants through the learning cycle from experience to application (also known as a Structured Experience). ELAs are carefully thought-out designs in which there is a definite learning purpose and intended outcome. Each step—everything that participants do during the activity—facilitates the accomplishment of the stated goal. Each ELA includes complete instructions for facilitating the intervention and a clear statement of goals, suggested group size and timing, materials required, an explanation of the process, and, where appropriate, possible variations to the activity. (For more detail on Experiential Learning Activities, see the Introduction to the *Reference Guide to Handbooks and Annuals*, 1999 edition, Pfeiffer, San Francisco.)

GAME A group activity that has the purpose of fostering team spirit and togetherness in addition to the achievement of a pre-stated goal. Usually contrived—undertaking a desert expedition, for example—this type of learning method offers an engaging means for participants to demonstrate and practice business and interpersonal skills. Games are effective for team building and personal development mainly because the goal is subordinate to the process—the means through which participants reach decisions, collaborate, communicate, and generate trust and understanding. Games often engage teams in "friendly" competition.

ICEBREAKER A (usually) short activity designed to help participants overcome initial anxiety in a training session and/or to acquaint the participants with one another. An icebreaker can be a fun activity or can be tied to specific topics or training goals. While a useful tool in itself, the icebreaker comes into its own in situations where tension or resistance exists within a group.

INSTRUMENT A device used to assess, appraise, evaluate, describe, classify, and summarize various aspects of human behavior. The term used to describe an instrument depends primarily on its format and purpose. These terms include survey, questionnaire, inventory, diagnostic, survey, and poll. Some uses of instruments include providing instrumental feedback to group members, studying here-and-now processes or functioning within a group, manipulating group composition, and evaluating outcomes of training and other interventions.

Instruments are popular in the training and HR field because, in general, more growth can occur if an individual is provided with a method for focusing specifically on his or her own behavior. Instruments also are used to obtain information that will serve as a basis for change and to assist in workforce planning efforts.

Paper-and-pencil tests still dominate the instrument landscape with a typical package comprising a facilitator's guide, which offers advice on administering the instrument and interpreting the collected data, and an initial set of instruments. Additional instruments are available separately. Pfeiffer, though, is investing heavily in e-instruments. Electronic instrumentation provides effortless distribution and, for larger groups particularly, offers advantages over paper-and-pencil tests in the time it takes to analyze data and provide feedback.

LECTURETTE A short talk that provides an explanation of a principle, model, or process that is pertinent to the participants' current learning needs. A lecturette is intended to establish a common language bond between the trainer and the participants by providing a mutual frame of reference. Use a lecturette as an introduction to a group activity or event, as an interjection during an event, or as a handout.

MODEL A graphic depiction of a system or process and the relationship among its elements. Models provide a frame of reference and something more tangible, and more easily remembered, than a verbal explanation. They also give participants something to "go on," enabling them to track their own progress as they experience the dynamics, processes, and relationships being depicted in the model.

ROLE PLAY A technique in which people assume a role in a situation/scenario: a customer service rep in an angry-customer exchange, for example. The way in which the role is approached is then discussed and feedback is offered. The role play is often repeated using a different approach and/or incorporating changes made based on feedback received. In other words, role playing is a spontaneous interaction involving realistic behavior under artificial (and safe) conditions.

SIMULATION A methodology for understanding the interrelationships among components of a system or process. Simulations differ from games in that they test or use a model that depicts or mirrors some aspect of reality in form, if not necessarily in content. Learning occurs by studying the effects of change on one or more factors of the model. Simulations are commonly used to test hypotheses about what happens in a system—often referred to as "what if?" analysis—or to examine best-case/worst-case scenarios.

THEORY A presentation of an idea from a conjectural perspective. Theories are useful because they encourage us to examine behavior and phenomena through a different lens.

TOPICS

The twin goals of providing effective and practical solutions for workforce training and organization development and meeting the educational needs of training and human resource professionals shape Pfeiffer's publishing program. Core topics include the following:

Leadership & Management

Communication & Presentation

Coaching & Mentoring

Training & Development

E-Learning

Teams & Collaboration

OD & Strategic Planning

Human Resources

Consulting